The
WILDFLOWER
BOOK

EAST OF THE ROCKIES

*Indeed, are they not all riddles? Where is the flower which even
to the most devoted of us has yet confided all of its mysteries?*
WILLIAM HAMILTON GIBSON, *Eye Spy*, 1897

STOKES NATURE GUIDES

BY DONALD STOKES

A Guide to Nature in Winter
A Guide to Observing Insect Lives
A Guide to Bird Behavior, Volume I

BY DONALD AND LILLIAN STOKES

A Guide to Bird Behavior, Volume II
A Guide to Bird Behavior, Volume III
A Guide to Enjoying Wildflowers
A Guide to Animal Tracking and Behavior

BY THOMAS F. TYNING

A Guide to Amphibians and Reptiles

STOKES BACKYARD NATURE BOOKS

BY DONALD AND LILLIAN STOKES

The Bird Feeder Book
The Hummingbird Book
The Complete Birdhouse Book
The Bluebird Book
The Butterfly Book

ALSO BY DONALD STOKES

The Natural History of Wild Shrubs and Vines

The
WILDFLOWER
BOOK

EAST OF THE ROCKIES

An Easy Guide to Growing and Identifying Wildflowers

DONALD and LILLIAN STOKES

Little, Brown and Company

Boston   Toronto   London

First Edition

Library of Congress Cataloging-in-Publication Data

Stokes, Donald W.

    The wildflower book : east of the Rockies : an easy guide to growing and identifying wildflowers / Donald and Lillian Stokes. — 1st ed.

       p. cm.

    Includes bibliographical references and index.

    ISBN 0-316-81786-4

    1. Wild flower gardening — United States.   2. Wild flowers — United States.   I. Stokes, Lillian Q.   II. Title.

SB439.S88   1992

635.9'676'0974 — dc20   92-12903

10 9 8 7 6 5 4 3 2 1

RRD-OH

Published simultaneously in Canada by Little, Brown and Company (Canada) Limited

Printed in the United States of America

Photograph Acknowledgments

Kathleen and Lindsey Brown: 6, 52 bottom, 54 bottom, 55 bottom, 90 top.

Alan Charnley: 11 bottom, 16, 59, 67 top, 68 bottom, 70 bottom, 73, 79, 86 bottom, 87, 93 top.

Raymond Coleman: 8, 34, 43 top, 50, 76 top, 77, 78, 80 top, 89 bottom.

Priscilla Eastman: 64 top.

Barbara Gerlach: 66.

John Gerlach: 1, 23, 29 top left, 29 top right, 47 top, 65, 75, 83, 84 middle.

Jessie M. Harris: 24, 43 bottom, 48, 49, 61, 62 bottom, 82 top, 88 top, 89 top.

Michael Havelin: 86 top.

George Humphries: 22.

Joseph Kayne: 27.

Paul Lindtner: 10, 55 top, 56 top, 58 bottom, 62 top, 64 bottom, 67 bottom, 88 bottom.

Adrienne McGrath: 84 bottom, 85 top.

Maslowski Photo: 37.

Ed Monnelly: 7, 17, 72 bottom.

New England Wildflower Society: Hal Horwitz — 11 top, 29 bottom right, 30 bottom left; Dorothy S. Long — 14.

Photo/Nats: Liz Ball — 74 top; Priscilla Connell — 81 bottom; Jean M. Fogle — 42; Don Johnston — 72 top; Lee Landau — 21; Bill Larkin — 82 bottom; Dorothy S. Long — 71 top; John A. Lynch — 29 bottom left, 52 top, 56 bottom; Jeff March — 80 bottom; Mary Nemeth — 53; Herbert B. Parsons — 60 top; David M. Stone — 54 top, 63, 68 top, 93 bottom.

C. Gable Ray: 20, 36, 45, 70 top.

John Shaw: 32 right, 33.

Leroy Simon: 71 bottom.

Rob and Melissa Simpson: 26 right, 28, 30 top, 30 bottom right, 31, 35.

Lee Snider: 92.

Stokes Nature Company: 12, 13, 15, 25, 38, 39, 40, 41, 58 top, 85 bottom.

John L. Tveten: 46 bottom, 47 bottom, 81 top.

Visuals Unlimited: Joel Arrington — 74 bottom; W. Banaszewski — 91; Scott Berner — 18–19; Barbara Gerlach — 51; John Gerlach — 32 left, 44 top, 69, 90 bottom; Lucy Jones — 57 bottom; Kirtley-Perkins — 44 bottom; Joe McDonald — 46 top; W. Ormerod — 57 top; Nada Pecnik — 9, 26 left; Leonard Lee Rue III — 84 top; Richard Thom — 76 bottom; Dick Thomas — 60 bottom.

Contents

THE ROMANCE OF WILDFLOWERS

As Children

For many of us our love of wildflowers began when we were children. We wandered in sunlit meadows and were captivated by the colors, shapes, and scents of the beautiful flowers around us. We watched with curiosity as fuzzy bumblebees gathered pollen, and we ran after butterflies that flew from blossom to blossom as they sipped nectar, the liquid gift of the flowers.

Oxeye daisy.

We also played games with wildflowers, games that magically predicted our fortunes and future: pulling the petals off a daisy one by one to reveal the true feelings of a loved one while chanting "She loves me, she loves me not"; studiously holding buttercups under our chins to see if we liked butter as much as we already knew we did; or blowing on dandelion seedheads and counting the seeds that remained to tell us the time of day or how many children we would have.

In addition, there were the childhood crafts with wildflowers. We wove chains of daisies and clovers into necklaces, bracelets, and garlands to grace our hair. And occasionally, our small hands gathered bouquets of wildflowers to be presented with pride to those we loved.

As Adults

As adults, most of us still enjoy wildflowers. We search along woodland paths for the earliest treasures of spring, and we are thrilled by the sight of a colorful midsummer meadow. We photograph and paint wildflowers, we arrange cut wildflowers in summer, and we dry wildflowers in fall for winter arrangements. And many of us attempt to grow them on our own property in whatever places they seem to thrive. In short, as adults we try to surround ourselves with wildflowers, indoors and out, in as many ways as we can.

This book has been written to help enrich your experience with wildflowers. There are chapters on growing wildflowers in woodland or meadow settings. We show how to incorporate them into existing perennial gardens or use them as landscape elements to conserve water or attract wildlife. We

Field with black-eyed Susan, yarrow, purple loosestrife, blanket-flower, Queen Anne's lace, red clover, and deptford pink.

teach you how to grow, preserve, dry, and arrange wildflowers for your home. We explain how to conserve wildflowers. And we provide a picture gallery of favorite eastern wildflowers filled with identification clues, cultivation information, and fascinating lore.

We hope this book will help you to fill your life with wildflowers. In so doing, you can bring together the beauty, magic, and romance of wildflowers that you felt as a child with the knowledge and abilities that you have as an adult.

Happy "wildflowering."

Don and Lillian Stokes

WILDFLOWER CONSERVATION

The Ecological View

As the human race matures in its understanding of ecology, it becomes increasingly clear that to save species of plants and animals we must save a critical mass of their environments. Nothing lives in isolation from other things; everything is interconnected.

This is especially true of wildflowers. Many of our native species are dwindling in number as human activity diminishes or destroys their environments. The prairies are a good example; they used to cover millions of acres in the Midwest, but now there are only a few areas where they can be seen. Accordingly, many of the plants that grew in them are now rare in the wild.

Thus, we must conserve the species *and* the habitats in which they live. To paraphrase the pioneer conservationist Aldo Leopold, "A good tinkerer never loses any of the parts." As we "tinker" with the environment, we should be sure not to lose any of the species that are a part of it.

It is equally true that on a larger scale each habitat is an irreplaceable part of the whole organism we call earth. This view of the earth as an organism is the next step humans need to take and one we are on the threshold of accomplishing.

Some people point out that we need to save wildflowers for the things that they may be able to offer medicine or industry, as if their use to humans is the main reason to save them. An even more important reason is that they are an integral part of our habitat. And when our own habitat is endangered our survival is in jeopardy.

What Can We Do?

There is no need to feel helpless when it comes to preserving wildflowers, for there are many easy steps that each of us can take, some right in our own backyards.

The first thing to do is join your local wildflower or native plant society. These organizations need your support, and they will also sensitize you to the conservation needs of your area.

Next, look closely at your own backyard. You may be surprised by what is already growing there. We have a swampy area on our property that we rarely venture into, but when we went in to look

Yellow lady's slipper.

A forest floor covered with white trillium.

it over, we found Canada lilies, Jack-in-the-pulpits, and false hellebore already growing there.

In addition to discovering plants, you will most probably want to introduce some additional wildflowers on your property, no matter how small it is. Wildflower gardening is sometimes considered a special sort of hobby, but it is really no different from other gardening; it just happens to focus on native plants. You may want to augment the wildflowers that are already growing at the edge of your lawn; you may want to add wildflowers to a woodsy place where many other plants have trouble growing; or you may want to make a complete wildflower garden or meadow.

Where to Get Wildflowers

If you want to grow wildflowers on your property, you will need to acquire them first. People used to collect plants from the wild, but today this is frowned upon by conservationists. Even when you buy plants from a nursery, you should ask the owner if the plants were nursery-propagated or dug from the wild. In almost all cases, lady's slippers and trilliums are dug from the wild. You can help preserve wildflowers by being a choosy shopper and only buying plants from those nurseries and native plant societies that propagate their own wildflowers. (Contact your local native plant society for recommended nurseries, or send for the list

compiled by the New England Wildflower Society — see Resources, page 94. The wildflowers in this book that are most often dug from the wild are identified in the index.)

In addition, do not pick wildflowers indiscriminately, for this can damage the plants and reduce their seed production. And always ask permission before picking flowers from private or public land. Feel free to pick from your own garden, but in the wild, remember that every picked flower means fewer seeds for maintaining that species.

Native Versus Alien

Native wildflowers are species that grow and reproduce in a particular place and were not brought there by humans. *Alien* plants are species that evolved in different habitats or regions and were brought to the new area either inadvertently or on purpose by humans.

The concept of native versus alien is important in wildflower conservation, since habitats are often delicately structured and the introduction of an alien species can upset that structure by crowding out native plants. As you grow wildflowers, continue to increase your awareness of which are native and which are alien. By favoring native species on your property, you can aid in preserving the diverse and complex habitats upon which we all depend.

WOODLAND WILDFLOWER GARDENS

Wildflowers at Their Best

Many of the native wildflowers that we love best in eastern North America evolved in a wooded environment. Because of this, they are tolerant of shade and tend to bloom early in spring before the leaves on the trees emerge. The rest of the year, only the leaves and stems are visible and, in the case of the spring ephemerals, not even that, since their leaves die back in midsummer, and only the root system remains to keep the plant alive until the next growing season. This is why the best time to go out and see woodland wildflowers is in early spring.

Wild columbine.

Picking a Site

There are two ways to pick a site for your woodland wildflowers. One is to go around your property and look for a place with the right conditions; the other is to pick a good potential location in which you want woodland wildflowers to grow and slightly alter it until it meets the right requirements.

An ideal site for woodland wildflowers is in rich soil under tall deciduous trees that let dappled light filter down to the ground. Water should not collect on the site, but neither should it be bone dry; and the acidity of the soil should be fairly neutral.

If your chosen site does not have enough light, then you may want to consider removing one or two trees or trimming the lower branches or thinning the crowns of the existing trees. The amount of moisture in the soil and the texture, organic content, and acidity of the soil can be changed later (see "Preparing the Soil," below). The amount of rainwater that gets to the area is harder to regulate without changing the topography of the land.

Planning the Garden

Once you pick the site, you can have the fun of planning your garden. Laying a garden hose on the ground to show the outlines of paths and beds is an easy way to get a sense of how you want to configure your garden beds. Consider creating a path to walk on while you enjoy your wildflowers. You also might want a bench somewhere along the path, facing your favorite view of the garden.

When planning the garden, take into account the heights and blooming times of the plants, with small plants in the front and taller ones toward the back, and with something in bloom during each month of the growing season. Whenever possible, try to create masses of color and foliage by planting groups of each species.

A woodland wildflower garden with yellow lady's slipper and blue phlox.

The Best and Easiest Plants for Starting a Woodland Garden

The Easiest to Grow

Bloodroot — *Sanguinaria canadensis*
Blue phlox — *Phlox divaricata*
Canada anemone — *Anemone canadensis*
Creeping phlox — *Phlox stolonifera*
Foamflower — *Tiarella cordifolia*
Green and gold — *Chrysogonum virginianum*
Jack-in-the-pulpit — *Arisaema triphyllum*
Mayapple — *Podophyllum peltatum*
Solomon's seal — *Polygonatum biflorum*
Virginia bluebells — *Mertensia virginica*
Wild bleeding heart — *Dicentra eximia*
Wild columbine — *Aquilegia canadensis*

Other Good Plants to Grow

Bluebell — *Campanula rotundiflora*
Closed gentian — *Gentiana andrewsii*
Crested iris — *Iris cristata*
Forget-me-not — *Myosotis scorpioides*
Round-lobed hepatica — *Hepatica americana*
Snakeroot — *Cimicifuga racemosa*
Spring beauty — *Claytonia virginica*
Squirrel corn — *Dicentra canadensis*
Violets — *Viola*
Wild geranium — *Geranium maculatum*

If you do make a path, try to mark the beginning and end of it with a bolder statement, such as a shrub, a special planting, or a large rock on either side. Paths can be lined with small rocks or old logs to give them more definition and then covered with pine needles, wood chips, crushed stone, pebbles, or bark mulch.

Preparing the Soil

First of all, try to get a sense of your existing soil by digging out a shovelful from various spots in each proposed flower bed. If you have numerous rocks, try to remove as many as you can. Small rocks can be used to line an edge of the garden and large ones can be lifted to the surface and used as a design element in the bed by placing plants in a pleasing relationship to them.

If your soil is divided up or crisscrossed by large roots, then just work with the pockets of soil between them and let spreading plants trail artfully over them.

Wild geranium.

Next, take a handful of the soil from your future beds and check its texture. Soils have three main textures: *sandy* soil feels gritty and is composed of sand-sized particles; *clayey* soil feels smooth or greasy and is made of extremely fine particles; and *loamy* soil contains a mixture of fine and sandlike particles. An easy measure of texture is to take a handful of soil and try to squeeze it into a lump. If it totally falls apart, it is too sandy; if it forms one solid clump, it is too clayey; and if it forms a clump that breaks apart into several smaller clumps when you release it, it is loamy. Almost all plants grow better in loamy soil.

Woodland plants also prefer soil with lots of organic matter, often called *humus*. Humus is decayed animal and plant matter in the form of compost, peat moss, manure, or leaves or shredded bark that has begun to rot. Humus adds essential nutrients and water-absorbing capacity to the soil of a woodland garden.

You can improve sandy soil by adding humus. And you can correct clay soils by adding sand and humus. In either case, be sure to loosen and mix your soil by turning it over with a fork or a small Rototiller before planting.

The last thing to check is the soil's pH, how acid or alkaline it is. The pH scale measures the concentration of hydrogen ions in the soil (*pH* stands for "potential of hydrogen"), and ranges from 1 to 14. A pH of 7 is neutral; less than 7 means acid soil, more than 7 means alkaline. Most woodland plants prefer soil that is just about neutral or slightly acid; some need a more acid soil. To test your soil, go to the nearest nursery and buy a small testing kit. They are easy to use and are a good general indicator of pH.

When you know the pH of your soil, you have two choices on how to proceed. You can choose plants that will like your soil just as it is, e.g., acid-loving plants for acidic soil, or you can change the soil to match the plant's requirements. If you want to change your soil and it is too acidic, you can add to it either lime — 5 pounds of ground limestone per 100 square feet will bring the pH of your soil from 5.5 to 6.0 — or compost, which will also help raise the soil's pH. If your soil is too alkaline, you can add sulfur — 2 pounds of sulfur per 100 square feet will bring the pH from 8.0 to 7.0 — or you can add peat moss or rotted pine needles, which will help make the soil more acid.

Planting Wildflowers

Now the real fun begins, deciding which plants you want and where they will go. Woodland wildflowers should be bought from reputable dealers who

Preparations for a garden of woodland wildflowers — enriched earth beds, background plantings of laurels and rhododendrons, and a path covered with wood chips and lined with old logs.

Green and gold blooming in a woodland setting.

you are sure do not dig them from the wild, or given to you by friends who divide wildflowers from their own garden. You should never dig plants from the wild except in cases where they will be destroyed by the construction of a road or building, and even then you must have permission of the landowner. For nurseries that carry native plants, see Resources, page 94.

As you select plants, be aware of their growth habits. Some species, such as Canada anemone, bergamot, and creeping phlox, spread aggressively. Give these plants room to spread and plant them in places where they will not interfere with other plants. Other species may readily self-sow, and you will need to plan room for their offspring. The Gallery of Favorite Wildflowers, starting on page 42, tells you about the growing habits of many plants.

When buying plants, get three or more of each species so that you can create masses of the same leaves and flowers, and create natural-looking groups. Look at the lists in this chapter for some of the easiest plants with which to start.

It is good to have your wildflower garden close to a source of water, for you will need to water the plants during dry spells. Water them individually with a hose in the morning. Using a sprinkler is not as effective; it gets the leaves wet, and its droplets often run off the soil surface. If you have a large garden, you may have to use a sprinkler, and in this case, mulch on the ground keeps the water from running off.

Mulching and Maintenance

Once you have planted and watered your wildflowers, it is a good idea to consider putting a mulch over the bare areas between plants. Mulches serve many important functions: they hold in moisture; they keep weeds from growing; they prevent erosion; they protect the soil from the heat of the midday sun and the cold of the night air; and as they decompose they add humus to the soil.

There are a variety of effective mulches. Several layers (5–10) of newspaper laid over the bare ground and then covered by a thin layer of bark mulch works well and will decompose by the same time next year.

Natural materials for mulching include pine needles (for acid-loving plants), bark mulch, old wood chips (not fresh), chopped-up leaves (one of the best), and dried grass clippings (if they are mixed with other organic material).

If any weeds do grow, they should be pulled up before they have time to go to seed. After a year or two you may want to divide certain plants that have grown a great deal and replant them in other parts of your garden or give them to a friend just starting out.

CREATING WILDFLOWER MEADOWS

The Dream

Flowering meadows are among the most beautiful and romantic wildflower gardens. They evoke images of a carefree existence with clear days, butterflies, picnics, and children picking wildflower bouquets.

These scenes can be yours if you have the right conditions of sun, soil, and moisture and are willing to spend some time in starting and maintaining a meadow garden. All of us would love to have acres of flowering fields, but in reality, a wildflower meadow is a garden and needs continual care. Because of this it is probably best to start with a small area of 50 to 100 square feet and see how it goes.

Choosing a Spot

The first step in creating a wildflower meadow is choosing a location. As with other wildflower habitats, there are four things to check when choosing a spot: the amount of sun it gets, the amount of moisture in the soil, and the texture and acidity of the soil.

The main element needed for a meadow is sun, at least 6–8 hours a day. The more sun, the better the meadow will grow.

Next, dig up a shovelful of soil and feel it. If it is gritty or sandy and light in color it should be enriched by the addition of humus. Humus is merely decayed vegetation such as compost or peat moss. If the soil is slippery and dense, it may be full of clay. Clay soils do not drain out moisture quickly, and most meadow wildflowers like a well-drained soil. To improve clay soil, add sand and humus. Most meadow wildflowers can survive in a wide range of soils and often do best in average to sandy soils.

Next, check your chosen area for moisture. Is the soil bone dry most of the time? Or is it damp at all times? In either case there are certain species that can tolerate these conditions better than others. See the lists on page 16 to match species to your type of soil.

Finally, you should check the pH of the soil. As explained on page 12, you can buy a kit at your garden center that will help you do this. Most meadow plants like neutral soils, or those at about 6–8 on the pH scale.

Black-eyed Susan, blazing star, and Turk's-cap lily.

A wildflower meadow mix with bachelor's button, blanketflower, black-eyed Susan, and cosmos predominant.

Three Ways to Create a Wildflower Meadow

How you go about creating your meadow depends on your property, the tools you use, and the amount of time you want to spend. The most color and greatest variety of flowers are created by sowing wildflower seeds; but this is also the most time-consuming approach. Slightly easier, but more expensive, is plugging plants into an existing grassy meadow. And the easiest and least expensive way is through varying your mowing practices on an existing field or meadow.

Method 1: Sowing Seeds

Wildflower meadows can be grown from seed, using a commercial mix or one that you design on your own. But you cannot just sprinkle wildflower seeds on unprepared soil and expect this to result in a gorgeous mass of wildflowers. The earth must be clear of weeds and other competing plants and

raked level so that seeds can get good contact with the soil for moisture and nutrients.

Preparing the Soil — There are three ways to prepare soil for seeds: 1) repeated rototilling; 2) rototilling followed by mulching; and 3) rototilling combined with the use of a "safe" herbicide (one that has a short life and low toxicity).

Rotary tilling is used in all three methods because it turns over and uproots existing vegetation, helping to kill it. In a small area you can turn over the soil by hand. For a slightly larger area you can buy or rent a small Rototiller. And in still larger areas you will need to hire someone with a tractor to turn over the soil.

In the first method, thoroughly rototill your area to about 6 inches deep; this may take 2–3 passes of the Rototiller. Then rake the soil, ideally when it is dry, to remove clumps of earth and plant litter and to make the soil surface smooth. After 2–3 weeks, do a shallow rototilling (1 inch deep) to kill

Blanketflower and coreopsis in a field.

come harmless in about 2–3 weeks. If, after 2–3 weeks, weeds and other plants still grow, reapply the herbicide. In any case, be sure to wait at least 2 weeks for the herbicide to break down before planting seeds.

Sowing Seeds — Before sowing seeds, mix them with slightly dampened sand. This keeps the different-size seeds evenly mixed and enables you to see where you have already sown. Mix 5 or more parts sand to each part seeds and dampen with water. Then take the seed-and-sand mixture and scatter it over the ground with a sweeping hand gesture as you walk back and forth over the meadow area.

Next, rake over the soil very lightly to cover most seeds with about ½ inch of soil. After this, tamp down the soil with a roller, with your feet, or with a board that you put down and step on.

Finally, water the seeds and try to keep the ground moist until many of the seeds have germinated, which should be within 1–2 weeks. If you do not have a source of water near your meadow, cover the area with a light mulch of seed-free grasses, such as salt marsh hay, or just hope for periodic showers.

other plants that may have grown. Repeat shallow rototillings each 2–3 weeks until you are satisfied that you have killed all or most of the weed seeds in the upper soil layer. Some people water their sites to encourage weed seed growth between rototillings.

The second method also starts with a deep rotary tilling and then raking of the soil. After this, the area should be covered with black plastic and left until fall if you started in spring, or until late spring if you started in fall. The dark plastic absorbs the sun's heat and kills growing plants underneath. After removing the plastic, plant wildflower seeds immediately.

The third method of soil preparation also starts with a thorough rototilling to a depth of 6 inches, followed by raking. After waiting 2–3 weeks for weed seeds or grass rhizomes to grow, spray the area with a glyphosate herbicide, such as Kleenup or Roundup, to kill actively growing plants. These herbicides are considered safe if used correctly, for they break down in the soil and be-

---

Some Easy-to-Grow Native Meadow Wildflowers

Dry Meadow Conditions

Black-eyed Susan — *Rudbeckia hirta*
Blanketflower — *Gaillardia aristata*
Blazing star — *Liatris spicata*
Butterfly weed — *Asclepias tuberosa*
Goldenrod — *Solidago canadensis*
New England aster — *Aster novae-angliae*
Purple coneflower — *Echinacea purpurea*
Sunflower — *Helianthus annuus*
Wild Lupine — *Lupinus perennis*

Moist Meadow Conditions

Bee balm — *Monarda didyma*
Canada lily — *Lilium canadense*
Fireweed — *Epilobium angustifolium*
Ironweed — *Vernonia noveboracensis*
Joe-Pye weed — *Eupatorium purpureum*
Queen-of-the-prairie — *Filipendula rubra*

A field filled with black-eyed Susan, Queen Anne's lace, yarrow, purple loosestrife, and oxeye daisy.

Weeding — When you see little sprouts first start to appear in your meadow area, you may not be able to tell if they are from the seeds you planted or just weeds. But as the plants grow, you may begin to recognize some as weeds, although this takes considerable experience. If you are sure, then start weeding your meadow.

How much you weed a wildflower meadow is up to you and is also affected by the size of your meadow. Since some so-called weeds are native wildflowers, you may want to leave them alone and let them add to your collection. On the other hand, if you have a small meadow and want just the species you planted, then you should look over your plants for weeds about once a week for the first 3 weeks after germination starts, and once every 2 weeks thereafter.

Changes over Time — Your wildflower meadow will change over time. In the first full year after planting, you will see mostly annuals bloom, for they live only 1 year. In this first year, the biennials (which bloom in their second year and then die) and the perennials (which keep blooming for several years) are growing roots and leaves. In the second year, they will dominate the wildflower meadow. Annuals will show up in the second year only if they find enough bare earth to grow from seeds they produced the first year. In the third year, your meadow may be almost all perennials. Grasses and other plants may also move into your meadow over the years.

Some people like the colors of annuals so much that they plant a mix consisting only of annuals each year. Even if you do not use only annuals, you may want to try a new wildflower mix in a year or two. In this case, just prepare the soil as before and sow new seeds over the old meadow area.

Choosing Wildflower Seed Mixes — There are many wildflower seed mixes available in stores and catalogs all across the country. These mixes can be broadly divided into two groups: specialty mixes and regional mixes.

Specialty mixes are for a certain effect or for a certain group of users. They include such categories as flowers that attract hummingbirds, butterflies, or birds; flowers for children; flowers for

Texas bluebonnets and Indian paintbrush in a roadside field.

Thistles and goldenrod.

shade or sun; flowers for moist or dry areas; and just annuals. Regional mixes are collections of seeds designed to be successful for a certain geographic region of the country, such as the Northeast, Mid-west, or Southeast. In some cases, mixes are both regional and specialized, such as northeastern annuals, or midwestern flowers for dry conditions.

Regional seed mixes from reliable companies are a good place to start because they contain wild-flowers proven to be successful in your climate and soil conditions. The next step is to read the labels on the packages and see what they tell you about the seeds. The more they tell you, the better you can judge the mix.

Here are some of the things you should look for when reading the label on a wildflower seed mix: the area of ground that the seed mix will cover; the scientific and common names of the flowers; which flowers are annuals, biennials, or perennials; and which plants are native. When comparing seed mixes, choose those with the greatest number of wildflowers native to your region. (For help in recognizing troublesome alien plants, see "Aggressive Alien Plants," at left.)

In addition, check to see if the mix contains any grass seeds. Grasses are an important part of a natural-looking meadow. However, some grasses spread rapidly and can crowd out wildflowers, while others form clumps that go nicely between the flowers. Species to avoid include tall fescue, annual rye, orchard grass, and Kentucky bluegrass. Clump-forming grasses that work well include little

Aggressive Alien Plants

Many of the plants in seed mixtures are not native to North America but were brought here by early settlers and explorers from Central America, Europe, Africa, and Eurasia. Some of these are particularly aggressive and can crowd out native species from certain habitats.

We recommend choosing a mix that has mostly native wildflowers and a minimum of the species listed below.

Bachelor's button — *Centaurea cyanus*
Bouncing Bet — *Saponaria officinalis*
Butter-and-eggs — *Linaria vulgaris*
Chicory — *Cichorium intybus*
Corn poppy — *Papaver Rhoeas*
Four o'clock — *Mirabilis jalapa*
Oxeye daisy — *Chrysanthemum leucanthemum*
Purple loosestrife — *Lythrum salicaria*
Queen Anne's lace — *Daucus carota*
Tickseed sunflower — *Bidens aristosa*
Yarrow — *Achillea millefolium*

Wild lupine.

bluestem, side oats grama, switchgrass, June grass, sheep fescue, Indian grass, blue grama, buffalo grass, and Indian ricegrass.

Method 2: Using Grown Plants

If you already have a meadow of grasses, an existing wildflower meadow, or just bare ground, you can add wildflowers by "plugging in" vigorous young plants. You can either buy these plants or grow them from seed and transplant them.

Buying even small wildflower plants is more expensive than sowing seeds, but it is a quick way to get results. When using grown plants, be sure to dig out a hole larger than the size of the pot your flower is in and fill the space with loose earth; this will keep the surrounding vegetation from immediately crowding it out and permits loose soil to make good contact with the plug.

The best way to grow wildflowers from seed for plugging is to use the plastic flats of 6–8 small (about 2 x 2 inches) compartments. Fill the compartments with potting soil and plant 3–4 wildflower seeds in each compartment. When the plants are several inches tall, or have well-developed rosettes (radiating clusters of leaves), you can easily remove them and transplant them safely. Maintain them by watering and keeping competing vegetation back.

Method 3: Through Mowing

If your chosen meadow area is covered by tall grass and possibly a few woody shrubs, take a closer look at it. Do you remember seeing any wildflowers here, such as buttercups, daisies, clovers, and other common species? At ground level, do you see any leaves or rosettes of plants other than grasses? Or have you just never looked very closely at this area through a spring and summer?

If the answer is yes to any of these questions, then you may already have a wildflower meadow and not know it. The way to tell for sure is to mow the area at distinct times and see if wildflowers bloom.

First, mow the area to not shorter than 6 inches in fall or early spring and then let it grow without mowing. Keep a list of all the wildflowers that bloom in the area. If, halfway through the summer, it is all grasses, then try mowing again and see if any wildflowers bloom in late summer or fall.

The reason we suggest this is that in most field areas there are many other plants growing, but they do not bloom because of competition with the grasses. By mowing in early spring and then in midsummer, you give the competitive edge to the flowers, helping them get enough sun to grow tall and bloom.

Black-eyed Susan, phlox, yarrow, and fire pink making a colorful scene in a meadow.

In the 2-acre field on our property, we use a variety of mowing practices. We mow some areas low every 1–2 weeks and keep them as lawn. We let one area grow in spring because it is full of hawkweeds, which bloom then; when they are finished blooming we mow that area for the rest of the year. Another area grows an abundance of Queen Anne's lace; we stop mowing it in midsummer and have a wonderful show of these flowers. And yet another area has a good natural mix of daisy, winter cress, red clover, buttercup, aster, and thistle; we let this grow all summer and then mow in late fall when all blooming is finished. We leave the unmowed areas in rounded, irregular contours so that they look more natural.

There has not been enough research done to know exactly when to mow a meadow to get the most flowers; thus, we encourage you to experiment with your own field. Certainly, a wildflower meadow of this type is the easiest to maintain and in many ways the most natural.

Most lawn mowers can mow no higher than 4

inches and so cannot be used for mowing wildflower meadows. Here are some options for the average homeowner. On very small plots, just use grass clippers. On larger plots use a weed cutter that cuts vegetation with a spinning nylon cord. For areas of an acre or two, a small riding tractor-mower that can be set to 6 inches high is best. For still larger areas you may need a full-size tractor, or you may have to hire someone who owns one.

Maintaining Your Wildflower Meadow

It is a good idea to mow over your wildflower meadow every year, for this keeps woody plants from getting started. Mowing should be done at least 6 inches high, for this will not disturb the plants that overwinter as leafy rosettes. Again, normal lawn mowers usually cannot be set this high, so you may need to use a weed cutter or small tractor-mower.

Great Plants for a Prairie Garden

A prairie is about 60–85 percent grasses and the rest wildflowers. Below are some good species of grasses and wildflowers for starting a small prairie garden. For ways to buy these grasses and wildflowers, see Resources, page 94.

Grasses

Big bluestem — *Andropogon gerardii*
Indian grass — *Sorghastrum nutans*
Little bluestem — *Schizachyrium scoparium*
Prairie dropseed — *Sporobolus heterolepis*
Switchgrass — *Panicum virgatum*

Wildflowers

Black-eyed Susan — *Rudbeckia hirta*
New England Aster — *Aster novae-angliue*
Oxeye — *Heliopsis helianthoides*
Prairie coneflower — *Ratibida pinnata*
Prairie smoke — *Geum triflorum*
Purple coneflower — *Echinacea purpurea*
Queen-of-the-prairie — *Filipendula rubra*
Rough blazing star — *Liatris aspera*
Thread-leaved coreopsis — *Coreopsis verticillata*
Wild bergamot — *Monarda fistulosa*

Oxeye daisy, red clover, orange hawkweed, and king devil in a natural field setting.

In addition, you may want to keep a watchful eye on your meadow over the years to be sure that no undesirable weeds are getting into it.

Restoring or Creating Prairies

A prairie differs from a wildflower meadow in that it is a natural climax community of plants rather than a largely human-made successional stage. This means that, once established, it is self-perpetuating and cannot be invaded by new plants that change its character. This is unlike a meadow, which if left alone will gradually be invaded by shrubs and trees and end up as a forest.

A prairie is very complex and in special soil conditions in the Midwest may contain almost 300 species. Prairies also differ from wildflower meadows in that they contain mostly grasses and just a few flowers. Most prairies are 60–85 percent grasses.

Starting a little patch of prairie is done much the same way as starting a meadow — by clearing the ground of existing vegetation and planting seeds or plugging in mature plants. In the box on the facing page you will see some of the better plants for a prairie community. These plants are available through many of the nurseries listed in Resources, page 94.

XERISCAPING — CONSERVING WATER

Five Steps

Xeriscaping (pronounced *zer*-i-scap-ing) is a landscaping concept whose main objective is conserving water. Although xeriscaping originated in the West, where water conservation has always been an issue, it also applies to the East, where water is rapidly becoming scarce and more expensive. By taking a few sensible steps you can practically halve the amount of water needed to maintain your landscape.

Briefly, here are five ways to conserve water in your landscaping. First, plan your yard carefully, seeing where moisture and drought occur naturally and putting appropriate plants in each area. Second, improve soil in all plantings by adding humus in the form of compost or peat moss to help the soil retain moisture. Third, mulch bare ground between and around plants to retain moisture and keep down weeds that would compete for water. Fourth, limit lawn to where you really need it and replace other areas with good ground covers — like junipers (*Juniperus* spp.), sedums (*Sedum* spp.), and lilyturf (*Liriope* spp.) — that need less water. And fifth, select wildflowers that grow naturally in dry situations, for these will be the most successful as well as beautiful. Below we have listed wildflowers that are tolerant of dry conditions. By following these steps you will both have more success in landscaping and contribute to water conservation.

Fire pink is one of the wildflowers that can live in dry areas.

Wildflowers for Dry Areas

Alumroot — *Heuchera villosa*
Black-eyed Susan — *Rudbeckia hirta, R. fulgida*
Blanketflower — *Gaillardia pulchella*
Blazing star — *Liatris spicata*
Butterfly weed — *Asclepias tuberosa*
Curtis aster — *Aster curtisii*
Fire pink — *Silene virginica*
Foxglove beardtongue — *Penstemon digitalis*
Lance-leaved coreopsis — *Coreopsis lanceolata*
Prairie coneflower — *Ratibida pinnata*
Purple coneflower — *Echinacea purpurea*
Pussytoes — *Antennaria plantaginifolia*
Scaly blazing star — *Liatris squarrosa*
Scarlet sage — *Salvia coccinea*
Stonecrop — *Sedum ternatum*
Sundrop — *Oenothera fruticosa*
Sunflower — *Helianthus tomentosus*
Thread-leaved coreopsis — *Coreopsis verticillata*
Wavy aster — *Aster undulatus*
Wild bergamot — *Monarda fistulosa*
Yarrow — *Achillea millefolium*

WILDFLOWERS IN THE PERENNIAL GARDEN

Perennial Favorites

One of the most popular types of gardening is growing perennials. Many of the plants now used for this purpose, and readily available from nurseries and gardening catalogs, are in fact native American wildflowers (and their hybrids and cultivars). These wildflowers make wonderful additions to the traditional perennial garden and often grow to their best when given optimal conditions of enriched soil and adequate sunlight and moisture.

On our almost 5-acre property we have lots of wildflowers, many of which came with the property. Some we cultivate in wildflower meadows, some we grow in a woodland garden, and some are in our perennial borders.

Experimenting by placing native wildflowers in the perennial garden is one of our favorite pastimes. In the perennial border, they form beautiful combinations with one another and with other exotic or alien species. Appearing in the list below are some of the best wildflowers for perennial gardens. We hope you will be tempted to try them in your garden.

Wildflowers for Perennial Gardens

Bee balm — *Monarda didyma*
Black-eyed Susan — *Rudbeckia fulgida*
Blazing star — *Liatris spicata*
Blue lobelia — *Lobelia siphilitica*
Boltonia — *Boltonia asteroides*
Cardinal flower — *Lobelia cardinalis*
Coreopsis — *Coreopsis lanceolata, C. verticillata*
Ironweed — *Vernonia noveboracensis*
Maryland golden aster — *Chrysopsis mariana*
New England aster — *Aster novae-angliae*
New York aster — *Aster novi-belgii*
Oxeye — *Heliopsis helianthoides*
Phlox — *Phlox pilosa ozarkana*
Obedient plant — *Physostegia virginiana*
Purple coneflower — *Echinacea purpurea*
Queen-of-the-prairie — *Filipendula rubra*
Rose mallow — *Hibiscus moscheutos*
Snakeroot — *Cimicifuga racemosa*
Sundrop — *Oenothera fruticosa*
Veronicastrum — *Veronicastrum virginicum*
Wild blue indigo — *Baptisia australis*
Wild columbine — *Aquilegia canadensis*

Cardinal flower is a favorite for the perennial garden.

TRILLIUMS

Conserving Two Special Flowers

Of all the wildflowers in eastern North America, two stand out as being among the best-loved and most sought after: trilliums and lady's slippers. Unfortunately, their status in our hearts has endangered their status in the wild, for hundreds of thousands of trilliums and lady's slippers have been dug from the wild and put on sale in nurseries to the public.

This has two effects. One is that it seriously depletes the populations of these plants in various areas of their natural habitat. The other is that the plants are often doomed to die in garden settings due to poor digging procedures when they were taken from the wild, shock to the plant, and a lack of understanding of the biology and needs of these plants when they are put in gardens.

Thus, we recommend that you not buy lady's slippers or trilliums for your garden, for by doing so, you are almost assuredly supporting suppliers who dig plants from the wild and diminish the natural populations of these beautiful wildflowers. Only in a few exceptional cases will you find trilliums and yellow lady's slippers that have been propagated.

You may well ask, Why are there such problems with trilliums and lady's slippers, when many

One of the variations of white trillium seen in the wild.

A many-petaled variation of white trillium.

A forest filled with white trilliums — *Trillium grandiflorum.*

other wildflowers are sold in nurseries? The main reason is that most other popular wildflowers can be grown economically from seed or from divisions of the plant. Lady's slippers cannot be grown successfully from seed, nor in most cases divided; and trilliums, although some can be grown from seed, take several years to reach blooming stage and are therefore too costly to raise and sell on a large scale.

Because of this, in this chapter and the following we describe the life histories and biology of these two special plants and picture the major species in each genus. Instead of trying to grow them in your garden, look for trilliums and lady's slippers in the wild — they are always more special and somehow magical in their natural setting.

Trilliums: From Seed to Flower

It can take 6–8 years for a trillium seed to result in a flower. It all starts with the seeds maturing in mid- to late summer. If the seeds remain moist, they will germinate the following spring, at which time all they do is develop a small root. They remain in this state through the next winter; the second spring, they produce a small, rudimentary leaf that pushes above ground and stays active for a month or two before dying back. Not until the plant is 3–5 years old does it produce a stem with the familiar 3 leaves.

But there is still longer to wait for the first flowers, for this flowerless 3-leaf stem is grown for 1 or 2 more years before flowers are produced. Thus, it takes a number of years for a trillium to produce its first flower.

Ants and Trillium Seeds

Trilliums are unusual in that ants play an important role in the dispersal of the plants. First, the seeds grow within a berrylike fruit. When mature, the fruit drops to the ground and splits open. The seeds

Dwarf trillium — *Trillium pusillum.*

are sticky, and attached to each one is a light-colored, oil-rich crest of material about the same size as the seed. This crest is called the strophiole, and one of its functions is to attract seed dispersers.

Ants, who explore every inch of the forest floor for food, find the seeds with attached strophioles and carry them toward their homes. At some point they detach the strophiole, which is what they want to eat, and leave the seed. Ants have been observed to carry trillium seeds as far as 30 feet from the plant. This is the main way that trilliums become dispersed throughout a forest.

Variations on a Theme

There are about 30 species of trilliums in North America. Most of these are indigenous to the East, and many are found only in the southern Appalachian Mountain area. Even though there are few species, identifying trilliums can be difficult, not only because some species look very similar, but also because some show a great deal of variation.

For example, white-flowered trillium (*Trillium grandiflorum*) is one of our most common trilliums and is generally easy to identify as having 3 large leaves without stalks and a large, 3-petaled white flower.

But many forms of this plant have been discovered over the years. In some, the leaves have stalks,

in others the leaves are stalkless. Still others vary in the number of leaves and petals, resulting in plants with leaves and petals in twos, threes, fours, and fives. In addition, blooms that start out white generally turn pink several days before the petals are shed. As if this were not enough, there are also forms with green-and-white-striped petals, all-green petals, or with some of the carpels and stamens (reproductive organs) in the center of the flower developing into petals in the form called *Trillium grandiflorum petalosum.*

Another common species, purple trillium, has a common name that belies its variety in the wild. Its flower can be crimson, purple, purple-brown, purple at the base and white further out, yellow, white, or green. This species may also have more than the usual 3 leaves, sepals, or petals.

A Trillium by Any Other Name

In addition to the variations of flower color and overall form in each species, there is quite a bit of confusion over common names.

All trilliums in the past have been referred to as wakerobins, a term probably given because trilliums bloom in spring at about the time robins nest. Currently, wakerobin most commonly refers to *Trillium erectum*. There are a bewildering number of other common names also applied to *T. erectum*,

Painted trillium — *Trillium undulatum*.

Purple trillium — *Trillium erectum*.

Toadshade — *Trillium sessile*.

Nodding trillium — *Trillium cernuum*.

Vasey's trillium — *Trillium vaseyi.*

Catesby's trillium — *Trillium catesbaei.*

Prairie trillium — *Trillium recurvatum.*

Yellow trillium — *Trillium luteum.*

including stinking Benjamin, stinking Willie, purple trillium, and red trillium, and there is a white form called white erect trillium. A widely accepted common name for *T. erectum* is purple trillium.

The name snow trillium has been used for 3 species: *T. grandiflorum, T. pusillum,* and *T. nivale.* It most properly belongs to *T. nivale* since *nivale* means "snow" and this species often blooms before the last snowfall.

There is also debate over the classification of trilliums and thus over their scientific names. There are several species of trilliums with flowers that sit directly upon the leaves and have no stalk. The most common species of this type is *T. sessile,* toadshade. Over the years there has been some question as to whether other, similar plants are actually separate species or merely variations on this main species. These other similar species are *T. cuneatum,* little sweet Betsy; *T. luteum,* yellow trillium; and *T. recurvatum,* prairie trillium.

As you find trilliums and try to differentiate between them, being aware of these variations in names will help you sort out and identify what you see.

LADY'S SLIPPERS

Protecting Lady's Slippers

As was said at the beginning of the previous chapter, lady's slippers should not be purchased from nurseries because the plants are almost certainly dug from the wild and this reduces natural populations. There is also a special characteristic of lady's slippers that makes buying them inadvisable, and that is that their roots need to be in close association with a fungus of the genus *Rhizoctonia* in order to properly supply the plant with nutrients. Lady's slippers usually lose this association in the process of being moved and rarely live more than a year or two after being transplanted.

We recommend that you look for the plants in the wild and enjoy their fascinating biology in their natural setting.

Long-Awaited Beauty

Lady's slippers are orchids, and thus their seeds do not develop like those of most other plants. In the case of the pink lady's slipper, thousands of seeds are shed in fall, each no bigger than a speck of dust. If a seed lands in an appropriate spot where all conditions are optimal, the next spring it swells and grows into a minute, hardened structure called a protocorm. The plant may remain like this until it is contacted by the *Rhizoctonia* fungus, which can take up to 2 years. The fungus acts like roots for the protocorm, helping it absorb nutrients from the surrounding soil so it can continue its growth. In 5–8 years the plant is large enough to produce a flower.

Showy lady's slipper.

Pink lady's slipper and its white form.

A spectacular group of pink lady's slipper.

How Many Species?

There are 6 main species of lady's slipper in eastern North America and some variations on each species. Below is a list of these species, with some clues to their identification and habitats and a description of their variations.

Pink Lady's Slipper — *Cypripedium acaule*. This is the most widespread of the lady's slippers. It is best distinguished from other lady's slippers by its leafless flower stem, which is unique to this species. It grows in a wide array of habitats, from dry, acid woods to hummocks and edges of bogs in the North. The single flower can range from light to dark pink. There is also an unusual form called *albiflorum*, in which the flower is white. This is easily distinguished from small white lady's slipper, which has leaves up the flower stem.

Showy Lady's Slipper — *Cypripedium reginae*. This species can be easily recognized by the color of its flower, which is generally white but suffused with a beautiful pink on its pouch, or "slipper." Showy lady's slipper may have 1 or 2 flowers per stalk. It is found in mossy swamps or woodland bogs and sometimes on limestone slopes. There is a white form called *albolabium*, meaning "white-lipped."

Yellow Lady's Slipper — *Cypripedium calceolus*. This is the only species with a yellow flower. There may be 1 or 2 flowers per stem. Sometimes there are varying amounts of spots of purple around the flower opening. There are 3 variations: var. *planipetalum*, which has flat sepals; var. *pubescens*, with twisted sepals; and the similar but smaller var. *parviflorum*.

Small White Lady's Slipper — *Cypripedium candidum*. This species is recognized by its all-white flower with a smooth and waxy appearance. Each stem has 1 (rarely 2) flowers. Unless they live in the Midwest, where this species is more common, most people who claim to have seen this species in the wild or have it growing in their gardens actually have the white form of the pink lady's slipper, which is easily distinguished by the lack of leaves on the stem and the slit for an opening in the front of the flower. The small white lady's slipper has leaves up the stem and an oval opening at the top of the flower. It is very rare.

Ram's-head Lady's Slipper — *Cypripedium arietinum*. This is also a very rare lady's slipper and has an unmistakable flower. It is only ½–¾ inch long and is triangular with the tip pointing down. It is white on top and veined with purple below. It has a slender stem and bluish-green leaves.

White lady's slipper.

Ram's-head lady's slipper.

Sparrow's-egg Lady's Slipper — *Cypripedium passerinum*. This species is small and has a white flower with purple spots on the inside and outside of the flower. It lives only in the conifer forests of eastern Canada.

Flower Fun House

The shape and colors of lady's slipper flowers seem unusual at first, until you understand the reasons for their design. Most flowers have evolved to attract pollinators and have these visitors carry pollen (the male sex cells of the flower) onto the female parts of the flower, where they can fertilize the eggs (the female sex cells of the flower) so they can develop into a seed. It is best if the pollen from one plant is transferred to the egg of another plant; this is called cross-pollination and it creates more chances for slight improvements in the plant.

Lady's slipper flowers do this cross-pollination

Yellow lady's slipper.

to perfection. Bees, the main pollinators, are first attracted to the openings of the lady's slippers. In all species but the pink lady's slipper, this is an oval opening on the upper side of the flower. In the pink lady's slipper, it is a slit on the front of the flower through which bees must push in order to enter. Once inside, the bees are attracted to an area of small hairs that excrete a sweet nectar in order to make the bees' efforts worthwhile. When the bee has finished eating, it starts to head out, but this is not easy. In the pink lady's slipper, the petals have closed behind the bee, and in the other species the openings curve down and in, so that as the bee crawls up it falls back. After realizing that there must be a better way, the bee sees the two small openings at the top of the flower where it is attached to the stem. As the bee crawls to one of these openings its back is scraped by a broad, flat surface with forward-pointing hairs. This is actually the female part of the flower, designed to

scrape off any pollen the insect may have brought from a previous flower. After this, the bee is then plastered on its back by the pollen holders and their sticky pollen. Finally it escapes, and believe it or not, it usually heads for another lady's slipper. That nectar inside must be *very* good!

In any case, the lady's slipper flower's little funhouse tunnel makes bees deposit pollen from a previous flower and carry new pollen to the next flower. This insures cross-pollination.

Sometimes larger bees cannot get out of the pink lady's slipper and end up chewing holes through the flower. In other cases, naturalists have found small butterflies called European skippers caught in pink lady's slipper flowers. These skippers evolved in Europe, outside the presence of lady's slippers, and are apparently unable to extricate themselves from this blossom, to which they are attracted by the colors and scent.

WILDFLOWERS FOR WILDLIFE

More Than Beauty

Beauty is not the only reward of planting wildflowers; there are also all of the birds and butterflies that the flowers attract. In fact, certain wildflowers are particularly alluring to butterflies, songbirds, or hummingbirds and, if you plant these, you have a good chance of tempting these delightful visitors into your yard.

Butterfly weed with an American copper on it sipping nectar.

Butterflies and hummingbirds come to flowers to drink the nectar in the blossoms. Although hummingbirds will feed at just about any flower that offers nectar, they are especially attracted to long, red, tubular flowers. The long tubes and horizontal or downward orientation of these flowers favor the hovering hummingbird with its long tongue and makes it hard for insects to land on the flower and reach the nectar.

Butterflies feed on a wide variety of wildflowers, but there are certain ones that they seem to love most. No one characteristic clearly distinguishes these flowers; they are just the ones at which observers have most often seen butterflies.

In addition to hummingbirds, your garden can attract other small birds, which come to eat the seeds or berries produced by the wildflowers. Finches, such as goldfinches, purple finches, and pine siskins, like seeds and often land on the flowerheads to feed. Other birds, such as juncos and a variety of sparrows, will feed on the seeds that have fallen from the flowers onto the ground. In our garden we leave flower stalks standing throughout winter, and we always find these species visiting those spots. Wildflowers that produce berries, such as baneberry and bunchberry, may attract fruit-eating birds, such as mockingbirds, cardinals, cedar waxwings, robins, and many others. Chipmunks will also feed on these berries.

When you see wildflowers attracting other wildlife, it is a reminder of the interconnectedness of nature. Wildflowers depend on their pollinators to enable them to produce seeds, and in turn the pollinators depend on the flowers' nectar as food. In addition, the berry-producing wildflowers count on birds to disperse their seeds as they eat the berries and void the seeds in new places.

The lists on the next page include wildflowers that attract birds and butterflies.

An American gold-finch feeding on the seeds of purple cone-flower.

Wildflowers That Attract Butterflies

Bee balm — *Monarda didyma*
Black-eyed Susan — *Rudbeckia* spp.
Blanketflower — *Gaillardia* spp.
Butterfly weed — *Asclepias tuberosa*
Coreopsis — *Coreopsis* spp.
Cosmos — *Cosmos bipinnatus*
Dame's rocket — *Hesperis matronalis*
Forget-me-not — *Myosotis sylvatica*
Gay-feather — *Liatris* spp.
Goldenrod — *Solidago* spp.
Hawkweed — *Hieracium* spp.
Ironweed — *Vernonia* spp.
Joe-Pye weed — *Eupatorium* spp.
Lily — *Lilium* spp.
Milkweed — *Asclepias syriaca*
New England aster — *Aster novae-angliae*
New York aster — *Aster novi-belgii*
Oxeye daisy — *Chrysanthemum leucanthemum*
Phlox — *Phlox* spp.
Purple coneflower — *Echinacea purpurea*
Queen Anne's lace — *Daucus carota*
Sneezeweed — *Helenium autumnale*
Sunflower — *Helianthus* spp.
Thistle — *Cirsium* spp.
Wild bergamot — *Monarda fistulosa*
Yarrow — *Achillea millefolium*

Wildflowers That Attract Hummingbirds

Bee balm — *Monarda didyma*
Cardinal flower — *Lobelia cardinalis*
Fire pink — *Silene virginica*
Fireweed — *Epilobium angustifolium*
Gay-feather — *Liatris* spp.
Indian paintbrush — *Castilleja coccinea*
Jewelweed — *Impatiens* spp.
Phlox — *Phlox* spp.
Wild bergamot — *Monarda fistulosa*
Wild bleeding heart — *Dicentra eximia*
Wild columbine — *Aquilegia canadenis*

Wildflowers That Attract Seed- or Berry-Eating Birds

Baneberry — *Actaea* spp.
Black-eyed Susan — *Rudbeckia* spp.
Bunchberry — *Cornus canadensis*
Clintonia — *Clintonia borealis*
Coneflower — *Ratibida* spp.
Coreopsis — *Coreopsis* spp.
False Solomon's seal — *Smilacina racemosa*
Jack-in-the-pulpit — *Arisaema* spp.
Purple coneflower — *Echinacea purpurea*
Spring beauty — *Claytonia virginica*
Thistle — *Cirsium* spp.

ARRANGING WILDFLOWERS

Double Pleasure

One of the most beautiful ways to enjoy and appreciate wildflowers is to go into your field or garden and gather bunches to fill vases and use in arrangements. Thus not only do your wildflowers provide you with the beauty of nature outdoors, but you also get the pleasure of having the lovely arrangements decorate the inside of your home.

Cut wildflowers can be enjoyed in both their fresh and dried states. We love to fill our home with fresh flowers during the summer growing season. In winter we dress up the house with a variety

An informal wildflower arrangement.

of beautiful dried arrangements and even incorporate dried flowers into the Christmas wreath we hang on our door.

Collecting Wildflowers

Although picking wildflowers may seem like a simple matter, there are some guidelines you should follow to protect the plants and make the task easier for yourself.

Only pick wildflowers from your own property or from other areas where you have the permission of the landowner. Do not pick wildflowers on public or protected lands (in some states it is illegal to pick wildflowers from along public roads). Do not pick endangered species (your State Natural Heritage Program will supply you with a list of endangered species in your region). Identify the species you are picking by using this guide or another wildflower guide. (See Resources, page 94.)

When gathering wildflowers, do not remove all the blooms from a plant; leave some blooms so the plant can set seed and reproduce. Never pull the plant up by its roots.

Cut the stem with a sharp knife or clippers, and remove any excess leaves or dead stalks. This is often done more easily on the spot than in your home. Place newly cut fresh flowers in a container partially filled with water. We find that a bucket or a plastic 1-gallon milk container with the top cut off makes a good carrying container.

Arranging Fresh Flowers

When you arrive home the creative fun begins as you decide how to use all the beautiful flowers. You may choose to make an informal bouquet by merely putting the flowers in a vase with water, or you might decide to design a more formal arrangement.

Fresh-cut wildflowers from our garden for an arrangement.

We keep a large collection of vases and containers of different colors and materials for just this purpose. It is fun to coordinate the colors of the flowers with those of the vase and then place the arrangement in just the right setting.

To make an arrangement you will need a block of "oasis," a foam brick that absorbs water and holds the flower stems in place. Soak the oasis in water for about ½ hour before using. Cut the oasis so that it fits inside the container and protrudes about 2 inches above it. Replenish the water in the oasis daily to keep the flowers fresh.

Cut flower stems at an angle — to absorb more water — and to the correct length for the arrangement you are creating. A general rule of thumb is to make the arrangement 1½ times higher than the container. Experiment with different forms and colors of flowers to see what pleases you. Flower arranging is an art that is mastered over time, and every time you make an arrangement you will learn something new.

Arranging Dried Flowers

Dried arrangements add beauty to your home in fall and winter and will last for many months. Making an arrangement with dried flowers is similar to making a fresh flower arrangement. However, dried arrangements do not require water, and this leaves you with a greater choice of containers. Be inventive. Baskets, seashells, pieces of driftwood, and many other objects can make wonderful containers for your dried flowers.

An oasis block is useful for dried arrangements also, for it holds the flower stems in place. Obviously, you should not soak the oasis before using it. Oasis foam bricks are available in brown as well as green, and the brown may blend better with dried arrangements. Handle the dried material carefully, since it is brittle and more fragile than fresh material. Consider using dried grasses and seedpods to add variety to your arrangements.

The next chapter explains how to dry flowers.

DRYING WILDFLOWERS

Lasting Treasures

Using dried wildflowers is an excellent way to bring beauty and color into your home all year round. A beautiful dried arrangement can dress up a table, serve as a centerpiece, or brighten a corner. Dried flowers can be used in wreaths and bouquets, and dried petals in potpourris. You can also press flowers and use them to make greeting cards, framed pictures, bookmarks, and other craft projects. You are limited only by your imagination.

Drying Flowers

Drying flowers is both easy and fun. First, collect flowers following the methods described in the previous chapter. Then strip most of the lower leaves off and remove any water or moisture from the stems, foliage, and flowers. From this point you have several methods of drying flowers from which to choose: hanging, drying flat, or using a desiccant.

A dried wildflower arrangement.

Hanging

Tie flowers of the same species in bunches by securing the bottoms of their stems with rubber bands. Hang the flowers upside down out of direct sunlight and in a dry place with good ventilation and air circulation. Do not make the bunches too large or hang them so closely together that air cannot adequately circulate. Bunches may be hung from coat hangers, drying racks, or from nails hammered into rafters. It takes flowers from several days to a week to dry by this method.

Drying Flat

You can also dry flowers by laying them flat on slatted shelves, trays with screen bottoms, or newspaper-covered trays. (Do not crowd the flowers on the trays.) Place trays in a warm, dry place. When thoroughly dried, the flowers should feel crisp. It takes flowers approximately 1 week to dry. This method works best for drying loose petals.

Additionally, flowers can be dried in about 1 hour when placed on a cookie sheet in an oven set to the lowest heat with the door propped open. This method should be used with extreme care and only by responsible adults.

Using a Desiccant

Finally, cut flowers may be dried by placing them in a desiccant, which is an absorbent powdery material such as silica gel or a mixture of 3 parts borax to 10 parts white cornmeal. Flowers dried in this manner retain their color and structure better than with other drying methods.

Silica gel, available from garden shops and florists, is the most expensive desiccant but is very effective and easily used. It can be reused indefinitely if dried out in an oven at low temperature after use. It turns white when it absorbs moisture but reverts to its blue color when dry.

When using a desiccant, remove stems from flowers to be dried. (They can be given false stems when dry by inserting florist's wire into the base

Materials for drying and pressing wildflowers: a drying rack, desiccant, and a flower press.

of the bloom.) Put a 1-inch layer of desiccant into an airtight container and lay the flowers on top. In general, lay blossoms faceup. Certain large blooms, like lilies, can be filled with desiccant first and placed faceup. Some flowers that are flat-petaled, like daisies, are best dried facedown.

Cover the flowers completely by gently pouring desiccant over them. Cover the container tightly and place it in a warm, dry place. Drying times vary from 2 days to 2 weeks, depending on the flower species. Flowers are done when they feel dry and papery.

Pressing Wildflowers

Pressed wildflowers make beautiful decorations. To press, gather wildflowers on a dry, sunny day when they are at their peak bloom. Select freshly opened, perfect blossoms. Flowers with heads that can be easily flattened work best. Some flowers press better when separated from their stems.

Press flowers between layers of good absorbent paper with firm and constant pressure for about 6 weeks. Old phone books are ideal because their paper is of the right absorbency and they contain many pages. Place as many flowers as will fit on a page and put several pages between each layer of flowers. Put weight, such as bricks, on the phone book to help press the flowers.

You also may purchase a flower press or construct your own. Use 2 pieces of plywood 9 inches square and ½ inch thick. Drill holes at each corner of the press and put 3-inch bolts through the holes and secure them with wing nuts. Press flowers in between 2 sheets of blotting paper (such as that used on desktops) and separate each layer of flowers from the next with a sheet of cardboard. Tighten the wing nuts to apply pressure to the sandwiched layers of flowers. Flowers take about 10 days to 6 weeks to dry.

Arrange pressed flowers in artistic combinations by gluing them on cards, bookmarks, or any kind of fabric or paper. Use a toothpick to apply a latex adhesive to the flowers. Protect your designs with clear varnish, acetate, coating resin, glass, or clear self-sticking adhesive covering film. Your creations will make beautiful and long-lasting treasures or gifts.

GALLERY OF FAVORITE WILDFLOWERS

The following section illustrates 87 favorite eastern wildflowers. The flowers are arranged by color, and within each color flowers with similarities are grouped together whenever possible. We start with three common but unusually colored flowers and then follow with this sequence: white, yellow, orange, red, blue, and pink.

To identify a flower in the field, look through the appropriate color section; to look up a flower for other information, use the index at the back of the book.

Accompanying each picture is text that describes lore, identification, habitat, range in eastern North America, origin, height, blooming period, and information on growing.

Some of the terms used in the sections giving identification clues may be unfamiliar to you; the glossary on page 94 defines many of them.

Each section of growing tips starts with the plant's light and soil requirements. The three categories of light we have used are *shade* (very little direct sun); *part shade* (dappled light or sun for less than 5 hours a day); and *full sun* (direct sun for 6 or more hours daily).

Soil can be classified according to four important qualities: texture, pH, organic content, and moisture. Most plants prefer a soil that has a loamy texture and is neutral in pH (pH 6.5–7.5). For a discussion of this, see "Preparing the Soil," page 10. Plants that have special pH requirements are so noted in the Gallery.

Organic content is the amount of rotted plant or animal material in the soil and can be roughly determined by the soil's color. Soil *low* in organic matter is poor soil, and its color is tan; *average* soil is moderate in organic matter and its color is brown; *rich* soil is filled with organic matter and is dark brown in color.

The moisture content of soil is determined by topography and by soil texture, with sandy soils draining rapidly and clayey soils holding moisture. We have divided soil moisture requirements into three types: *low* — soil is dry most of the time; *average* — soil is moist about half the time; and *high* — soil is usually moist.

Jack-in-the-pulpit — *Arisaema triphyllum*

JACK-IN-THE-PULPIT flowers are either male or female. Male flowers are usually on plants with just 1 set of 3 leaves; female flowers are on plants with 2 sets of 3 leaves, and they are the ones that produce the berries that turn bright red in fall. A given plant may change which sex flower it produces from year to year.

Identification clues: 1–2 large compound leaves, each with three leaflets; flower is green or purplish brown and looks like a pulpit with a person inside.

Where found: Moist woods; from Canada to the South. Native.

Height: 1–3 feet. **In bloom:** April–June.

Growing tips: *Light needs* — part shade; *soil needs* — average to rich organic content, average to high moisture. Produces flowers and fruits best when soil is rich and moist throughout the summer. Perennial.

Sᴋᴜɴᴋ ᴄᴀʙʙᴀɢᴇ is named for the odor of the leaves when crushed. The strange flower looks and smells like rotting flesh and attracts flies as pollinators; they are fooled into thinking it is a place to lay their eggs. The flower actually produces heat in early spring that melts any snow remaining about the bloom.

Identification clues: Large, strongly ribbed leaves, 1–3 feet long, emerging from the ground in wet areas; flower a reddish-green hood with a pollen-studded ball in the center; blooms before leaves emerge.

Where found: Swamps, wetlands, stream edges; from Canada into northern states and south into Appalachian Mountains. Native.

Height: 1–3 feet.   **In bloom:** February–April.

Growing tips: *Light needs* — part shade to shade; *soil needs* — rich organic content, high moisture. "Wet" is the key concept for this plant, for it can grow with its feet in the water. Left undisturbed in this condition it will grow as a clump and may even self-seed. Perennial.

Skunk cabbage — *Symplocarpus foetidus*

Canada wild ginger —
Asarum canadense

Wɪʟᴅ ɢɪɴɢᴇʀ is not related to the ginger from Asia that we use in cooking, but its roots do have a nice gingery odor. The flower is near the ground and pollinated by flies in early spring. It then develops into a leathery seed capsule, which eventually bursts apart, scattering the seeds.

Identification clues: A pair of heart-shaped, dark green leaves 3–6 inches wide; the single flower is reddish brown and is at the base of the plant.

Where found: Rich, moist woods; from Canada south to Arkansas and North Carolina. Native.

Height: 6–12 inches.   **In bloom:** March–May.

Growing tips: *Light needs* — part shade to shade; *soil needs* — rich organic content, average moisture. Mulching with rotting leaves in fall will help the plant for the following year. Spreads by rhizomes and by self-seeding. Perennial.

Bunchberry — *Cornus canadensis*

BUNCHBERRY is the diminutive relative of the flowering dogwood tree. Its leaves, flowers, and red berries are all similar to those of the tree, but bunchberry is only 3–5 inches tall. The "petals" of bunchberry are actually 4 leaflike bracts under a cluster of tiny 4-petaled flowers.

Identification clues: Six broadly pointed leaves in a whorl; center group of tiny flowers surrounded by 4 white "petals."

Where found: Cool, moist woodlands; from Canada south to the mountains of West Virginia. Native.

Height: 3–5 inches.   **In bloom:** May–July.

Growing tips: *Light needs* — part shade to shade; *soil needs* — rich organic content, average moisture. Will gradually spread through rhizomes and can form a ground cover, especially under evergreens. Red berries beautiful in fall and winter. Requires acidic soil (pH 5–6). Perennial.

DAISIES originated in Asia and spread from there to mainland Europe and then to England. They probably got to North America as seeds brought in the grain or hay carried on early colonists' boats. Oxeye daisies contributed to the hybrid we know as shasta daisy.

Identification clues: Leaves at base and on stem are narrow and have shallow lobes; each flowerhead has white ray flowers surrounding a center of yellow disk flowers.

Where found: Meadows, roadsides, waste spaces; from Canada south. Originally from Asia.

Height: 1–2 feet.   **In bloom:** June–August.

Growing tips: *Light needs* — full sun; *soil needs* — low to rich organic content, average moisture. Readily self-seeds, and seedlings can be easily transplanted. Divide in spring or fall. Perennial.

Oxeye daisy — *Chrysanthemum leucanthemum*

Water lily — *Nymphaea odorata*

WATER LILIES have floral movements, with the flowers opening about 11 A.M. and closing about 3 P.M. Once pollinated, the flower stays closed and the flower stem coils, pulling the developing fruits underwater. When they are ripe they burst and the seeds float to the surface and are dispersed to new areas.

Identification clues: Large circular leaves that float on the water surface; large white or pink flowers with many petals also floating on the water.

Where found: Ponds and lake coves; from Canada south. Native.

Height: 3–6 inches above water.

In bloom: June–September.

Growing tips: *Light needs* — full sun; *soil needs* — rich organic content, high moisture (under water). Purchased plants should be planted with roots buried in the mud at the bottom of a pond and held there with a rock. Will spread each year. Perennial.

BLOODROOT is named for the red juice within its rhizome. The seed pod splits open and releases the seeds, which are then sometimes collected by ants and carried off (the ant eats a nutritious area on the outside of the seed). The white flower closes each night until it is pollinated; then the petals are shed.

Identification clues: A single leaf wrapped around the plant stalk; large, single white flower about 2 inches wide on separate stalk.

Where found: Deciduous woods; from Canada south to Florida and Oklahoma. Native.

Height: 6–9 inches.　**In bloom:** April–May.

Growing tips: *Light needs* — full sun to shade; *soil needs* — average to rich organic content, average moisture. Mulch with leaves for winter. Leaves may die back in midsummer if there is drought. Will spread by rhizomes and may self-seed. Perennial.

MAYAPPLE is better known for its large leaves than its flower, for the flower, although lovely, is hidden beneath the umbrella of the two leaves. By midsummer, the flower has matured into a yellow, oval fruit about 2 inches long, from which the plant gets its common name. Plants are colonial, with interconnected, resource-sharing root systems.

Identification clues: Large leaves, a foot or more across, deeply lobed; a large white flower on a short stem at the base of the 2 leaves.

Where found: Moist, open woods; from Minnesota to southern New England and south. Native.

Height: 12–18 inches.　**In bloom:** April–June.

Growing tips: *Light needs* — part shade; *soil needs* — rich organic content, average moisture. Spreads quickly by rhizomes and can self-seed. Can form a wonderful ground cover under open deciduous woods. Perennial.

Mayapple — *Podophyllum peltatum*

White trillium —
Trillium grandiflorum

WHITE TRILLIUM, also called large-flowered trillium, is one of the most commonly grown trilliums in wildflower gardens. After being pollinated, the flowers start to change color from white to shades of pink. Trilliums, when started from seed, take 6–8 years to have their first bloom.

Identification clues: Three large pointed leaves at top of stem; large 3-petaled white flower, 2–4 inches across, is on a stalk. The flower points slightly upward.

Where found: Deciduous woods; from Maine to Great Lakes area and south to Georgia. Native.

Height: 12–18 inches. **In bloom:** April–June.

Growing tips: *Light needs* — part shade to shade; *soil needs* — rich organic content, low to average moisture. For best results, keep soil moist and mulch heavily with leaves each year. Will spread as a clump slowly. Perennial. *Note:* Almost all trilliums for sale are collected from the wild. If you want to buy one, be sure the nursery propagated it.

NODDING TRILLIUM is one of the more common species of trilliums to be found in the mid-Atlantic region. The flower is inconspicuous, for it is greenish white and hangs down. Nonetheless, it is visited by bumblebees who inadvertently pollinate it.

Identification clues: Three large pointed leaves at the top of stem; 3-petaled white flower is on a stalk and points down.

Where found: Woods; from Canada south into northern states, and further south in mountains. Native.

Height: 12–18 inches. **In bloom:** April–June.

Growing tips: *Light needs* — part shade to shade; *soil needs* — rich organic content, low to average moisture. For best results, keep soil moist and mulch heavily with rotted leaves each year. Will spread as a clump slowly. Perennial. *Note:* Almost all trilliums for sale are collected from the wild. If you want to buy one, be sure the nursery propagated it.

Nodding trillium — *Trillium cernuum*

Canada violet — *Viola canadensis*

CANADA VIOLET is just one of many violets that can be enjoyed in the wild and grown in your garden. Violets have some flowers that stay closed, self-pollinate, and develop seeds. The seeds of all violet flowers are shot from the pod as it dries and squeezes in on them.

Identification clues: Leaves toothed, heart-shaped, and attached to purplish stem that has fine hairs; flowers are white with a hint of purple on the back and are borne in the leaf axils.

Where found: Rocky woods; southern Canada and northern states, further south in Appalachian Mountains. Native.

Height: 10–15 inches. **In bloom:** April–July.

Growing tips: *Light needs* — part shade to shade; *soil needs* — rich organic content, average to high moisture. Will self-seed. Perennial.

FOXGLOVE BEARDTONGUE is called foxglove for its resemblance to the genus *Digitalis*, or foxgloves, and beardtongue because one of the 5 stamens in the flower does not have pollen and instead is covered with little hairs. The genus name, *Penstemon*, means "five stamens."

Identification clues: Leaves paired with no leaf-stalks; flowers white, tubular, with a large opening and 5 petals.

Where found: Fields, prairies, open woods; from northern states south in the East. Native.

Height: 3–5 feet.   **In bloom:** May–July.

Growing tips: *Light needs* — full sun to part shade; *soil needs* — average organic content, low to average moisture. Native penstemons do not need a lot of moisture and so are good for the water-conserving garden. They need to be replaced every 3–4 years to keep plants vigorous. Can self-seed under growing conditions mentioned here. Perennial.

Foxglove beardtongue — *Penstemon digitalis*

White turtlehead — *Chelone glabra*

TURTLEHEADS are named for their flower's resemblance to the head of a turtle. If you find the leaves of this plant eaten, it may have been done by caterpillars of the Baltimore butterfly, which lays clusters of crimson eggs on the undersides of the leaves.

Identification clues: Leafy stalk; large, white to light pink, snapdragon-like flowers along the tip. Pink turtlehead, *C. lyoni*, is similar but with deep pink flowers.

Where found: Edge of ditches, streams, and swamps; from Canada south. Native.

Height: 2–4 feet.   **In bloom:** July–September.

Growing tips: *Light needs* — part shade to full sun; *soil needs* — rich organic content, average to high moisture. Grows best in soil that is wet all summer, such as alongside a stream or in a wet ditch. Divide plants in spring or fall. Perennial.

Dutchman's breeches — *Dicentra cucullaria*

DUTCHMAN'S BREECHES is named for the form of the flower, which resembles a pair of white pants. The nectar is deep inside the flowers and only bumblebees, with their long tongues, can reach it through the flower opening. However, smaller bees may poke holes in the sides of the flower to "steal" the nectar and bypass pollinating the flower.

Identification clues: Sprays of finely cut leaves; little white flowers that look like an upside-down pair of pants.

Where found: Moist, rich woods; from Canada south to South Carolina and Nebraska. Native.

Height: 6–12 inches.   **In bloom:** April–May.

Growing tips: *Light needs* — part shade to shade; *soil needs* — rich organic content, average moisture. Leaves die back in summer. Easy to grow and will spread. Divide tubers in late spring to summer to propagate. Perennial.

Squirrel corn — *Dicentra canadensis*

SQUIRREL CORN is named for the many yellow spherical tubers on the root, which resemble kernels of corn and which are, in fact, eaten by mice and squirrels. All parts of the plant contain poisonous alkaloids, but there is no danger in smelling the strong fragrance of the flowers, which is reminiscent of hyacinths.

Identification clues: Flat sprays of finely divided leaves (almost identical to those of dutchman's breeches); heart-shaped flowers hanging off a short stalk.

Where found: Moist, rich woods; southern Canada south to Missouri and North Carolina. Native.

Height: 6–12 inches.　　**In bloom:** April–June.

Growing tips: *Light needs* — part shade to shade; *soil needs* — rich organic content, average moisture. Leaves die back in summer. Easy to grow and will spread. Divide tubers in late spring to summer to propagate. Perennial.

Canada anemone —
Anemone canadensis

ANEMONE'S white, petal-like structures are actually sepals, since the plant has no petals. This is why the flower looks so exquisitely simple. *Anemone* is a Greek word meaning "daughter of the wind." In early times, people believed it was pollinated by the wind or closed its blossoms in the wind. Neither is the case.

Identification clues: A whorl of 3 deeply lobed leaves at base of flower stalk; large white flowers, 1 per flower stalk.

Where found: Moist meadows, roadside ditches, the edges of lakes and streams; from Canada south to Georgia, Tennessee, and Kansas. Native.

Height: 1–2 feet.   **In bloom:** April–July.

Growing tips: *Light needs* — full sun to part shade; *soil needs* — low to rich organic content, average moisture. Will spread aggressively with rhizomes and self-seeding. Best planted where it will not crowd out other wildflowers, or controlled by planting in a sunken container. Division in spring or fall. Perennial.

Trailing arbutus — *Epigaea repens*

TRAILING ARBUTUS is also known as mayflower, for May is when its fragrant blooms appear. The flowers are pink or white, small, and often partially hidden among leaves, but they have an odor as sweet as a gardenia's and are visited by queen bumblebees as they start their brood in early spring.

Identification clues: Two-to-three-inch-long leathery, oval leaves along a trailing woody stem; flowers white, tubular at the base, and opening into 5 petals sometimes tinged with pink.

Where found: Deciduous woods with acid soil; from Canada south. Native.

Height: 2–4 inches.   **In bloom:** March–May.

Growing tips: *Light needs* — part shade; *soil needs* — rich organic content, average moisture. This is not an easy plant to grow or transplant and is mostly dug from the wild; therefore, we do not recommend you grow it. It needs acidic soil (pH 5–6) and must be kept moist all summer and mulched in winter to protect the evergreen leaves from drying out. Perennial.

Stonecrop — *Sedum ternatum*

STONECROP makes a lovely ground cover, especially if it is allowed to clamber over rocks on a wooded hillside, as its name suggests. It often prefers to grow in areas where limestone is present.

Identification clues: Small fleshy leaves in whorls of 3 on nonflowering stalks, leaves single and alternate on flowering stalks, flower with 5 sharply pointed petals.

Where found: Rocky hillsides and woods; from New York to Illinois and south. Native.

Height: 4–8 inches.   **In bloom:** April–June.

Growing tips: *Light needs* — part shade; *soil needs* — low to rich organic content, average moisture. Stonecrop seems to prefer well-drained settings, where it spreads by runners and can self-seed. Perennial.

Red baneberry —
Actaea rubra

RED BANEBERRY produces red berries in early fall. The berries are poisonous to humans but probably harmless to birds, which eat them and disperse the seeds in their droppings. White baneberry, *A. pachypoda*, has white berries with a black spot at their tips, and for this reason is also called doll's eyes.

Identification clues: Large compound leaves, each with many strongly toothed leaflets; a cylindrical cluster of small flowers at the tip of a thin flower stalk. White baneberry is similar in bloom, but it has thick flower stalks.

Where found: Woodlands with rich, moist soil; from Canada to West Virginia, Indiana, and Kansas. Native.

Height: 1–3 feet.   **In bloom:** April–June.

Growing tips: *Light needs* — part shade to shade; *soil needs* — rich organic content, average moisture. Starts blooming when 2–3 years old. Divide in spring or fall. Perennial.

YARROW leaves, in the past, were steeped in water to make a tea that supposedly could help cure, among other things, baldness and the common cold, although both maladies obviously persist. The dried seedheads are sometimes used as miniature trees on architects' models.

Identification clues: Finely cut, fernlike leaves at the base and along the flower stalk; dense, flat-topped cluster of flowers at tip of stem. Crushed leaves smell medicinal.

Where found: Fields, roadsides, waste spaces; from Canada south. From Europe.

Height: 1–4 feet.   **In bloom:** June–September.

Growing tips: *Light needs* — full sun to shade; *soil needs* — low to rich organic content, low to high moisture. Good for meadows, although can spread aggressively. A water-conserving species well adapted to poor soils. Divide in spring or fall. Perennial.

Yarrow — *Achillea millefolium*

FOAMFLOWER is ideal for the woodland wildflower garden, for it is tolerant of a variety of conditions, blooms a long time, and has leaves that remain green through most of winter in protected areas.

Identification clues: Maple-shaped leaves on stalks growing directly from the ground; separate flower stalk lined at the tip with delicate, feathery flowers.

Where found: Deciduous woods; from Canada south to Georgia mountains. Native.

Height: 6–12 inches.　**In bloom:** April–June.

Growing tips: *Light needs* — part shade; *soil needs* — rich organic content, average moisture. There are two variations: *T. cordifolia* var. *cordifolia* spreads by runners and makes a good ground cover; *T. cordifolia* var. *collina* stays in a clump and does not spread as much. Perennial.

Foamflower — *Tiarella cordifolia*

Queen Anne's lace — *Daucus carota*

QUEEN ANNE'S LACE, also called wild carrot, is the species from which present-day carrots were developed. The leaves, when crushed, smell like carrot leaves, and there is a tough, carrotlike taproot. Attractive dried winter seedheads open and close with changes in humidity.

Identification clues: Basal rosette of fernlike leaves in first 1–2 years; 2nd–3rd year grows a branching stalk with white, flat-topped clusters of flowers at the tips.

Where found: Fields, roadsides, waste spaces; from Canada south. From Europe.

Height 2–4 feet.　**In bloom:** June–September.

Growing tips: *Light needs* — full sun; *soil needs* — low to rich organic content, average moisture. Requires 2 years to flower and then dies, but can self-seed. Good for meadows and sometimes perennial gardens. Biennial.

Snakeroot — *Cimicifuga racemosa*

SNAKEROOT flowers are beautiful but have a foul odor that is designed to attract flies, which do snakeroot's pollination for it. Another lovely common name that describes the delicate nature of the blooms is fairy candles. *Cimicifuga* means "drives bedbugs away," as the leaves were believed to do.

Identification clues: Tall plants with compound leaves; flower spikes 1–3 feet long and covered with delicate white flowers.

Where found: Rich, moist woods; from Maine to Wisconsin and south to Georgia and Missouri. Native.

Height: 5–8 feet.   **In bloom:** June–September.

Growing tips: *Light needs* — part shade; *soil needs* — rich organic content, average moisture. May not flower until 3rd or 4th year after germinating. Enjoys being heavily mulched with rotting leaves. Perennial.

Galax — *Galax aphylla*

GALAX is a favored woodland wildflower that can be grown quite far north of its natural range. It is best in groups of several plants, forming a lush, evergreen scene. The delicate flowers rise up above the leaves on separate stalks and are beautiful in filtered light.

Identification clues: Rounded, shiny, evergreen basal leaves; flower stalk tall with small white flowers forming a point at the tip of the stalk.

Where found: Mountain woods; from Virginia south. Native.

Height: 1–2 feet.   **In bloom:** May–June.

Growing tips: *Light needs* — part shade to shade; *soil needs* — rich organic content, average moisture. Mulch with decaying leaves in winter. Can grow in acid soil. Divide pink rhizome in fall. Perennial.

FALSE SOLOMON'S SEAL has something to offer the wildflower lover throughout the growing season: in spring it has graceful arching stems with leaves; in summer it has showy flowers; and in fall it has a large cluster of bright red berries. A similar, smaller species is starry false Solomon's seal, *S. stellata,* whose berries, instead of being red, are dark red to maroon with black stripes.

Identification clues: Alternate, parallel-veined leaves on a slightly zigzag, arching stem; white flowers at the tip of the stem. Solomon's seal (*Polygonatum biflorum*) has similar stem and leaves but has flowers at each leaf axil.

Where found: Woods; from Canada south. Native.

Height: 1–3 feet.   **In bloom:** May–July.

Growing tips: *Light needs* — part shade; *soil needs* — rich organic content, average moisture. This plant prefers slightly acid soil but will grow under a variety of conditions. Good foliage plant in shaded locations. Spreads by growth of rhizomes. Perennial.

False Solomon's seal — *Smilacina racemosa*

Solomon's seal — *Polygonatum biflorum*

SOLOMON'S SEAL is named for the supposed resemblance of the leaf scars on the rhizome to the seal of King Solomon. These are graceful plants known more for the design of their leaves and their blue berries than for their small, inconspicuous, greenish flowers.

Identification clues: Alternate, parallel-veined leaves on an arching stem; small bell-like flowers hang mostly in pairs off the leaf axils.

Where found: Rich, moist woodlands; from Iowa to Connecticut and south. Native.

Height: 1–3 feet.   **In bloom:** May–June.

Growing tips: *Light needs* — part shade to shade; *soil needs* — rich organic content, average moisture. Spreads through rhizomes, and if happy will form a large grouping. Prefers slightly acid soil. A larger species, *P. commutatum,* needs constantly moist ground to flourish. Perennial.

Green and gold — *Chrysogonum virginianum*

GREEN AND GOLD is a wonderful flower for the dappled sun of woodland gardens, since it is easy to grow, spreads rapidly, and is green through winter. It is one of the earliest members of the daisy family to bloom in spring.

Identification clues: Low, evergreen leaves; yellow, daisylike flowers with 5 outer ray flowers.

Where found: Moist, shaded woods; mid-Atlantic states south. Native.

Height: 6 inches.

In bloom: April–October.

Growing tips: *Light needs* — full sun to part shade; *soil needs* — low to rich organic content, average moisture. Does best in rich soils, where it can spread through rhizomes and self-seeding. Makes a nice ground cover. Perennial.

COMMON SUNDROP is in the genus of evening primroses. The plants of this genus can be roughly divided into two groups: those that open their blooms in the evening (evening primroses) and those that open their blooms during the day (sundrops). This is the most common species of sundrop, but there are many others and they sometimes hybridize. A shorter species is Missouri primrose, *O. missouriensis.*

Identification clues: Smooth, lance-shaped leaves alternate along stem; flowers yellow with 4 petals, a pistil in the form of a cross, and orange stamens.

Where found: Fields and meadows; from Canada south. Native.

Height: 1–3 feet.

In bloom: June–August.

Growing tips: *Light needs* — full sun; *soil needs* — average organic content, low to average moisture. Spreads to form a clump. Can be divided in spring or fall. Overwinters as a reddish rosette. Perennial.

Common sundrop — *Oenothera fruticosa*

Marsh marigold —
Caltha palustris

MARSH **MARIGOLD** is one of the loveliest flowers of wet areas, putting on a show of yellow blossoms in spring that rivals that of any other wildflower. No wonder it is so popular with photographers and gardeners alike.

Identification clues: Glossy, heart-shaped leaves; bright yellow buttercup-like flowers.

Where found: Wet areas and swamps; from Canada south to South Carolina and Nebraska. Native.

Height: 6 inches–2 feet.   **In bloom:** April–June.

Growing tips: *Light needs* — full sun to part shade; *soil needs* — rich organic content, average to high moisture. After blooming, leaves die back and plant becomes dormant, at which time it can be divided. Will self-seed. Perennial.

Canada lily — *Lilium canadense*

CANADA LILY is a strikingly beautiful native plant that can be a wonderful addition to your garden. Place it at the back of the garden, since it is tall and this may also protect its thin stems from being bent by the wind.

Identification clues: Very tall plant with whorls of leaves along the stem; up to 12 yellow to red to orange, bell-like flowers hanging downward.

Where found: Moist meadows and swamps; from Canada south to Alabama and Georgia. Native.

Height: 2–6 feet.   **In bloom:** July–August.

Growing tips: *Light needs* — full sun to part shade; *soil needs* — rich organic content, average to high moisture. You will have to purchase plants, since growing them from seed is a delicate procedure and it can take up to 4 or 5 years to get blooming plants. Check to be sure plants you buy are propagated and not dug from the wild. Can be propagated in late summer by detaching the smaller bulbs from the main bulb. Perennial.

Clintonia — *Clintonia borealis*

CLINTONIA is named for DeWitt Clinton, who was once the governor of New York and was also an avid naturalist. The plant is also called bluebead lily due to its parallel-veined leaves and dark blue berries.

Identification clues: Large shiny leaves at the base; a leafless flower stalk topped by greenish-yellow bell-like flowers.

Where found: Moist, cool woods, brushy bogs; from Canada south to the Carolinas and Georgia mountains. Native.

Height: 6–15 inches.   **In bloom:** May–June.

Growing tips: *Light needs* — shade; *soil needs* — rich organic content, high moisture. Prefers acidic soil. Difficult to grow, for they need the specific conditions of their natural environment. They do not transplant well. Perennial.

Trout lily — *Erythronium americanum*

TROUT LILY'S leaves are long, pointed, and mottled with brown, making them look like a trout under the ripples of a mountain stream. The plants also often grow near streams and bloom when the trout season is about to begin.

Identification clues: One or 2 long thin leaves mottled with purplish brown; a single flower stalk with a yellow, lilylike flower.

Where found: Open woods, thickets, streamsides; from Canada south. Native.

Height: 6–12 inches.   **In bloom:** March–May.

Growing tips: *Light needs* — shade; *soil needs* — rich organic content, high moisture. Best grown near a stream or other spot where it is always moist. Plants take 4–7 years of growing until they bloom. From then on may bloom sporadically. In late summer, side bulbs can be detached from mature bulbs and planted nearby to increase your stand. Perennial.

Yellow iris — *Iris pseudacorus*

YELLOW IRIS was imported to North America from Europe and escaped from gardens in numerous areas of the country. It now can be found growing wild along ponds and wetlands. In the Middle Ages iris became the heraldic symbol for the royalty of France; it was called the fleur-de-lis.

Identification clues: A tall iris in wet locations with yellow blossoms about 2 inches across.

Where found: Streams and lake edges, marshes; from Canada south. From Europe.

Height: 2–4 feet.   **In bloom:** May–July.

Growing tips: *Light needs* — full sun to part shade; *soil needs* — rich organic content, high moisture. This is a very hardy plant that can thrive if planted at the edge of a lake, pond, or stream. It needs to stay wet or moist at its base and will spread gradually over the years, even with no special attention. Some consider it invasive in the wild, so keep it confined to the garden. Perennial.

CELANDINE POPPY is often confused with celandine, which is also in the poppy family but in a different genus. Celandine poppy has flowers twice as large — up to 2 inches across.

Identification clues: Large, gray-green, deeply cut leaves arranged opposite on the stem; large, 4-petaled yellow flowers at base of leaves.

Where found: Rich, damp woods; from Wisconsin to Pennsylvania and south. Native.

Height: 10–15 inches.   **In bloom:** March–May.

Growing tips: *Light needs* — full sun to part shade; *soil needs* — rich organic content, average moisture. The plant will benefit from added humus in the soil, being kept moist in summer, and being mulched in winter. Will self-seed. Perennial.

Celandine poppy — *Stylophorum diphyllum*

Lance-leaved coreopsis — *Coreopsis lanceolata*

Lance-leaved COREOPSIS is popular among gardeners, for it is easy to grow and spreads at a moderate rate. *Coreopsis* means "looks like a bug" and refers to the small seeds.

Identification clues: Lance-shaped leaves sometimes with 2 extra lobes at the base; all-yellow, daisylike flowerhead.

Where found: Fields, roadsides; from mid-Atlantic states south. Native.

Height: 1–2 feet.   **In bloom:** June–August.

Growing tips: *Light needs* — full sun; *soil needs* — average organic content, low to average moisture. Will spread through rhizomes, forming a large clump. Can be divided in spring or fall if the plant appears to be too crowded. Perennial.

Sunflower — *Helianthus annuus*

SUNFLOWERS come in several sizes; the wild species have smaller flowerheads, while the cultivated species can have flowerheads up to a foot across. Goldfinches, chickadees, and titmice love to eat the nutritious seeds right off the plant. Sunflower seed is the most popular ingredient in birdseed mixes.

Identification clues: Tall with alternate leaves that are broad and pointed at the tip and have rough surfaces; large flower with yellow ray flowers and a center of brown disk flowers.

Where found: Roadsides, fields, waste spaces; from Canada south. Native.

Height: 3–12 feet.   **In bloom:** July–October.

Growing tips: *Light needs* — full sun; *soil needs* — low to rich organic content, average moisture. Easy to grow and will tolerate dry, poor soils. Needs to be replanted from seed each year. Annual.

Oxeye — *Heliopsis helianthoides*

OXEYE looks a lot like a sunflower but in fact is not in the same genus. Instead of producing seeds with kernels in them like the sunflower, it produces achenes, which are dry, hard seeds that do not split open.

Identification clues: Leaves short and in pairs along the smooth stem; sunflower-like flowerheads.

Where found: Streamsides, meadows, and waste spaces; from Canada south. Native.

Height: 3–5 feet.   **In bloom:** July–September.

Growing tips: *Light needs* — full sun; *soil needs* — low to rich organic content, average moisture. Can grow in dry, poor soils. Spreads only slightly, forming a dense clump. Perennial.

Prairie coneflower —
Ratibida columnifera

CONEFLOWERS are named for the tall central portion of the flowerhead, which is conelike. There are two related species: *R. pinnata* has a cone shorter than its ray flowers, and *R. columnifera* has a cone longer than its ray flowers.

Identification clues: Divided leaves with deep, narrow lobes; yellow ray flowers bent back and a tall brownish cone in the center that is composed of disk flowers.

Where found: Prairies, roadsides, waste spaces; throughout Midwest from Canada to Mexico. Native.

Height: 3–4 feet.   **In bloom:** June–August.

Growing tips: *Light needs* — full sun; *soil needs* — low to rich organic content, low to average moisture. This plant is tolerant of dry soil and will develop a dense root system, making it hard to divide. Once established, it can spread. Perennial.

Hawkweed —
Hieracium pratense,
H. aurantiacum

HAWKWEEDS were named for the belief that the plant could help your eyesight and make your vision as good as that of a hawk. People thought that even hawks came down to the plant and used the sap to better their eyesight.

Identification clues: A basal rosette of lance-shaped leaves with fine hairs on them; separate, leafless flower stalk topped by several yellow or orange dandelion-like flowerheads. Yellow flowers indicate king devil, *H. pratense;* orange flowers indicate rocange hawkweed, *H. aurantiacum.*

Where found: Roadsides, sparse fields, lawns; from Canada south into Appalachian Mountains. From Europe.

Height: 1–3 feet.   **In bloom:** May–September.

Growing tips: *Light needs* — full sun; *soil needs* — average organic content, low to average moisture. Hawkweeds do well where other vegetation is sparse, for this enables the basal rosette to get sunlight. Spread by rhizomes that put up new rosettes. Perennial.

BLACK-EYED SUSAN is native to the prairies but moved east when settlers made roads to the Midwest, for the roadsides became sunny openings in the woods in which the plants could grow. The genus is named for a famous Swedish botanist, Olaf Rudbeck.

Identification clues: Short hairs on leaves and stem; flowers with long yellow ray flowers and a rounded brown center of disk flowers.

Where found: Fields, roadsides, waste spaces; from western New England to Minnesota and south. Native.

Height: 2–3 feet.   **In bloom:** June–October.

Growing tips: *Light needs* — full sun; *soil needs* — low to rich organic content, average moisture. Can be grown from seed and will start blooming in the 2nd year. Will bloom for 1–3 years and then need to be replaced. Short-lived perennial.

Black-eyed Susan — *Rudbeckia hirta*

Goldenrod — *Solidago* spp.

GOLDENRODS are late-season plants perfect for a wildflower meadow. They attract myriad insects, which come to feed on the abundant pollen and nectar. The pollen from goldenrod does not cause hay fever, as is commonly believed, since it is sticky and rarely gets airborne.

Identification clues: There are many species of goldenrod and they are not easy to distinguish. All have strong, tall stems with bright yellow flowers clustered at the tips. Flowers tend to be arranged along the tops of the branches off the main stem.

Where found: Meadows, fields, roadsides; from Canada south. Native.

Height: 1–5 feet.   **In bloom:** July–October.

Growing tips: *Light needs* — full sun to part shade; *soil needs* — low to rich organic content, average moisture. Goldenrods are tough plants that live in moist or dry situations. They form a dense clump, which can be divided. Will self-seed. Perennial.

Turk's-cap lily — *Lilium superbum*

TURK'S-CAP LILY, under the right conditions, can produce up to 50 blooms on a single plant — definitely a superb sight. Although the flowers are pendant, the ripened seed capsules point up and split along their sides to let seeds be blown short distances by the wind.

Identification clues: Tall stalks with whorls of leaves; petals and sepals of flower strongly curved back and green at the base, then yellow, then orange and spotted throughout.

Where found: Wet meadows and swamps; from southern Canada south. Native.

Height: 4–8 feet.   **In bloom:** July–August.

Growing tips: *Light needs* — part shade; *soil needs* — rich organic content, average to high moisture. Bulbs should be planted 4–8 inches beneath the soil surface in fall. Mulch in summer and keep moist. May need to be protected from wind or staked. Perennial.

JEWELWEEDS get their name from the silvery drops of dew seen at the tips of the leaves in the morning, or from the way their flowers hang like earrings off the branches. They are also called touch-me-nots because if you touch the seedpods when they are just about ripe, they explode and shoot the seeds out to disperse them.

Identification clues: A large plant with many succulent branches and stems; flowers hang from the branch tips like miniature cornucopias. Orange flowers are spotted jewelweed, *I. capensis;* yellow flowers are pale jewelweed, *I. pallida.*

Where found: Streamsides, lakesides, wet ditches, wetlands; from Canada south. Native.

Height: 2–5 feet.   **In bloom:** July–October.

Growing tips: *Light needs* — part shade; *soil needs* — average to rich organic content, average to high moisture. This large plant is an annual and so must sprout from seed each year. Seeds can be collected from the plant and spread over moist, open ground. Once established it will self-seed. Annual.

Spotted jewelweed — *Impatiens capensis*

Wood lily —
Lilium
philadelphicum

WOOD LILIES are a favorite of wildflower enthusiasts everywhere. They are not common in the woods and when found are almost shocking in their beauty and size. They are sometimes pollinated by tiger swallowtail butterflies, which get pollen on the tips of their wings when reaching down to get the nectar.

Identification clues: Unlike the blossoms of most other wild lilies, the wood lily's blossom faces straight up; it is orange with dark spots inside.

Where found: Meadows and woodland clearings; from Canada south to North Carolina and Nebraska. Native.

Height: 1–3 feet.   **In bloom:** June–July.

Growing tips: *Light needs* — part shade; *soil needs* — rich organic content, average moisture. Bulbs should be planted 4–5 inches deep in spring or fall. Can be propagated in late summer by detaching the smaller bulbs from the main bulb. Almost all of these lilies available to buy are dug from the wild; be sure the ones you buy are nursery-propagated. Perennial.

Butterfly weed — *Asclepias tuberosa*

BUTTERFLY WEED is one of the best flowers for attracting adult butterflies. They cannot resist the large amounts of nectar in this plant's lovely orange blossoms. Look for little bags of pollen — the plant's means of pollination — stuck to the butterflies' feet.

Identification clues: Long, narrow, hairy leaves; clusters of bright orange flowers at the tips of stems; flowers also sometimes red or yellow; no milky juice in stems.

Where found: Sandy areas, dry fields, roadsides; from Canada south to the Gulf of Mexico. Native.

Height: 1–3 feet.

In bloom: June–September.

Growing tips: *Light needs* — full sun to part shade; *soil needs* — low to average organic content, low moisture. The soil must be well drained, otherwise roots will rot. Once it is established, leave it alone and just enjoy it. Best grown from seed. Perennial.

INDIAN PAINTBRUSH, with its red, tubular flowers, is perfectly adapted for hummingbird pollination and can be an important source of nectar for wild birds. Pollen travels from flower to flower on the foreheads of hummingbirds that visit the plants for nectar.

Identification clues: Spikes of red flowers are actually red, 3-lobed bracts around greenish-yellow tubular flowers.

Where found: Meadows, prairies, sandy soils; from Canada south. Native.

Height: 1–2 feet.   **In bloom:** June–August.

Growing tips: *Light needs* — full sun to part shade; *soil needs* — rich organic content, average moisture. Not easy to grow. Needs time to become established. Indian paintbrush may attach its roots to those of other plants to help it grow. Perennial.

Indian paintbrush — *Castilleja coccinea*

BEE BALM got its common name from the belief that the leaves could ease the pain from bee stings. It is also called Oswego tea, for the Oswego Indians steeped the leaves in hot water to make a satisfying drink. It is a good plant for attracting hummingbirds.

Identification clues: Square stem and opposite, toothed leaves; red, tubular flowers clustered at the nodes at the top of the stem.

Where found: Streamsides, wet meadows; eastern United States south to Georgia and Tennessee. Native.

Height: 3–5 feet.

In bloom: June–August.

Growing tips: *Light needs* — full sun to part shade; *soil needs* — average to rich organic content, average to high moisture. Spreads rapidly through a thick mat of roots that should be divided every 2–3 years. Perennial.

Bee balm — *Monarda didyma*

Blanketflower — *Gaillardia aristata*

BLANKETFLOWER is extremely tolerant of dry soil conditions and thus is ideally suited to gardening styles that put a premium on conserving water. Blanketflowers bloom throughout summer and also make good cut flowers, lasting longer if cut before the bloom fully opens.

Identification clues: Large daisylike flower with a center of reddish disk flowers encircled by ray flowers that are red near the center and yellow at the tips.

Where found: Plains, prairies, dry hillsides; from northern Midwest to Northwest, spreading east. Native.

Height: 8–24 inches.   **In bloom:** June–September.

Growing tips: *Light needs* — full sun; *soil needs* — average organic content, low to average moisture. Divide in spring every 2–3 years to keep plants vigorous and increase your stock. Perennial.

Fire pink — *Silene virginica*

FIRE PINK is a striking sight in its native haunts, for its bright red blossoms contrast so with the rocks and gravel in which it often chooses to grow. The red, tubular flowers are very attractive to the ruby-throated hummingbird, which becomes a regular visitor in the summer as it gathers nectar.

Identification clues: Opposite, lance-shaped leaves on a sticky stem; flowers deep scarlet with 5 notched petals.

Where found: Rocky woods, open hillsides, roadside banks; from Minnesota to New Jersey and south. Native.

Height: 1–2 feet.   **In bloom:** April–June.

Growing tips: *Light needs* — full sun to part shade; *soil needs* — average organic content, low to average moisture. Can survive in gravelly soil but can do spectacularly in good soil with mulch, watering, and fertilizer. Divide every 1–2 years for vigorous specimens. Perennial.

WILD COLUMBINE flowers are pollinated by hummingbirds. They are red and have long tubes at the end of which are little storage places for nectar. As hummingbirds hover beneath them to sip nectar, they get pollen on their faces, which they then carry to the next flower.

Identification: Small, lobed leaves in groups of 3; hanging red flower is distinctive.

Where found: Often in rocky areas of woods, cliffs, or slopes; from Canada south. Native.

Height: 1–3 feet.

In bloom: April–July.

Growing tips: *Light needs* — full sun to part shade; *soil needs* — average organic content, average moisture. Do not overfertilize or you will get mostly leaves. Mature plants can lose vigor in 3–4 years and need replacing. Will self-sow. Perennial.

Wild columbine — *Aquilegia canadensis*

CARDINAL FLOWER is one of the favorite flowers of ruby-throated hummingbirds. It is the one flower in our yard that hummingbirds actually fight over. Although most individual hummingbirds extract nectar from the front of the flower, some reach the nectar by poking a hole through the base of the blossom.

Identification clues: Alternate lance-shaped leaves along single stem; deep red, tubular flowers along the tip of the stem.

Where found: Along slow-moving rivers and streams, in wet meadows; from the northern states south. Native.

Height: 2–4 feet.

In bloom: July–September.

Growing tips: *Light needs* — full sun to part shade; *soil needs* — average organic content, average to high moisture. Grow in a moist area of your property that gets about half a day of sun. Rhizomes produce offshoot rosettes in fall, and these can be separated and planted elsewhere to increase the number of plants. Self-seeds in moist conditions. Perennial.

Cardinal flower — *Lobelia cardinalis*

Purple trillium — *Trillium erectum*

PURPLE TRILLIUM is also frequently called wake-robin, possibly because it grows and blooms when robins return to their breeding grounds. It is one of the more variable of trilliums in its flower color, for it can range from purple to red to pink to white.

Identification clues: Three large pointed leaves at the top of stem; 3-petaled red flower is at the tip of a stalk.

Where found: Moist deciduous woods; from Michigan to Quebec and south to Pennsylvania, further south in the Appalachian Mountains. Native.

Height: 12–18 inches. **In bloom:** April–May.

Growing tips: *Light needs* — part shade to shade; *soil needs* — rich organic content, average moisture. For best results, keep soil moist and mulch heavily with rotted leaves each year. Will spread slowly as a clump. Perennial. *Note:* Almost all trilliums for sale are collected from the wild. If you want to buy one, be sure the nursery propagated it.

Creeping phlox —
Phlox stolonifera

CREEPING PHLOX is just one of the many native phloxes that can be grown in your garden. It produces delicate blooms for a long period of time, and as its spreading branches touch the ground, they produce new roots at that spot and continue to grow.

Identification clues: Sprawling stems with small paired leaves; flowers light blue with 5 petals and a long tube. There are many other phloxes with similar blossoms, such as sweet William, *P. maculata,* and blue phlox, *P. divaricata.*

Where found: Moist woods and bottomlands; from Pennsylvania to Ohio and south to South Carolina and Georgia. Native.

Height: 6–12 inches.   **In bloom:** April–June.

Growing tips: *Light needs* — part shade; *soil needs* — rich organic content, average moisture. In these conditions, creeping phlox is an excellent garden flower, for it spreads rapidly and several plants can form a superb ground cover within a year or two. Readily self-seeds. Perennial.

Bluet — *Houstonia caerulea*

BLUETS close their flowers each night and droop over as the tip of the fine, hairlike stem bends. In the morning they open again and are often visited by special flies that look like bumblebees, called beeflies. *Bluet* means "small blue" in French.

Identification clues: Small basal leaves; flower small, 4-petaled, blue to white, with a yellow center.

Where found: Fields, roadsides, lawns; from Canada south. Native.

Height: 2–8 inches.

In bloom: April–July.

Growing tips: *Light needs* — full sun to part shade; *soil needs* — low to rich organic content, average moisture. Often found in poorer, gravelly soils where other plants are not growing. May die back in summer and then grow new rosettes in fall. Spreads by rhizomes that send up new rosettes of leaves. Perennial.

Forget-me-not — *Myosotis scorpioides, M. sylvatica*

FORGET-ME-NOTS are welcome additions to any garden, be it formal or wild. The two species mentioned here are from Europe and have escaped from gardens. Many other species are native to North America, but they are not encountered as often. *Myosotis* comes from Greek words meaning "mouse ear," referring to the small leaves of some species.

Identification clues: Familiar small, light blue flowers with 5 petals and a yellow center.

Where found: Streamsides, wet meadows, wet woods; from Canada south. From Europe.

Height: 6–12 inches.   **In bloom:** May–August.

Growing tips: *Light needs* — full sun to part shade; *soil needs* — average to rich organic content, average to high moisture. *M. sylvatica* is an annual; it readily self-seeds in areas with moist soil and blooms in spring. It is a good plant to fill in between other, later-growing plants in your garden. *M. scorpioides* is a perennial and also does best in rich, moist soil. Annual and perennial.

Bottle gentian — *Gentiana clausa*

BOTTLE GENTIAN looks like no insect could ever enter it, but bumblebees do, first with their head and then the front portion of their body, keeping their back portion and legs outside the narrow passageway to help them pull out. There is lots of nectar inside since no other insects seem strong enough to get in.

Identification clues: Clusters of upright, deep blue blossoms stay closed at the tips.

Where found: Streambanks, wet meadows, wooded slopes; from Canada south. Native.

Height: 1–2 feet. **In bloom:** August–October.

Growing tips: *Light needs* — full sun to part shade; *soil needs* — average organic content, average moisture. Grown from seed they take 2–3 years to first blooming. Easily grown. Divide roots in spring or fall to propagate. Perennial.

VIRGINIA BLUEBELL can be found thriving in large masses in the broad floodplains of large rivers. They do equally well in gardens. In the 1800s they were taken to England, where the famous landscape and garden designer William Robinson praised their beauty and said they should be more widely cultivated.

Identification clues: Large oval leaves, primarily along base of stem; loose clusters of trumpet-shaped flowers at top are pink as buds and blue as blossoms.

Where found: Moist woodlands, streamsides; from northern states south. Native.

Height: 1–2 feet. **In bloom:** April–June.

Growing tips: *Light needs* — part shade; *soil needs* — average to rich organic content, average to high moisture. Mulch in spring and keep moist. Plant dies back in early summer and will emerge again the following spring. Best left undisturbed once established. An easy plant to grow in a wildflower garden, and it self-seeds. Perennial.

Virginia bluebell — *Mertensia virginica*

HEPATICAS are lovely evergreen plants whose blooms open in early spring; some say it is the earliest flower to bloom. There are two common species, distinguished by the shape of their leaves: round-lobed hepatica and sharp-lobed hepatica, *H. acutiloba*.

Identification clues: Three-lobed evergreen leaves at the tips of thin, hairy stalks; flowers on separate stems have 6–10 petals and vary in color from white to pink to blue.

Where found: Rocky hillsides, open woods; from Canada south to Florida and Missouri Native.

Height: 4–6 inches. **In bloom:** March–May.

Growing tips: *Light needs* — part shade; *soil needs* — rich organic content, average moisture. Prefers slightly acidic conditions, where it will slowly spread. Can be divided in fall if then mulched. Eventually makes a good ground cover. New leaves appear after flowers bloom. Perennial.

Round-lobed hepatica — *Hepatica americana*

Fringed gentian — *Gentiana crinita*

FRINGED GENTIAN has the deepest blue blossoms of all our wildflowers. They are open when it is sunny but close during cloudy weather and at night to protect their pollen and nectar from rain or dew. The plant is uncommon in the wild, and its flowers should not be picked nor the plant dug up.

Identification clues: Upright blue, tubular flowers with petals opening at the top with fringe on their edges.

Where found: Lakesides, wet meadows, roadside ditches; from Canada south through the Appalachians and west into Ohio and Indiana. Native.

Height: 1–3 feet. **In bloom:** August–November.

Growing tips: *Light needs* — full sun; *soil needs* — rich organic content, average moisture. Fringed gentian is a biennial and so only blooms in its second year and then must be started over from new seed. Hard to start from seed, for seeds must be kept continually moist. During first year is a rosette. Once established, may self-seed. Biennial.

Blue-eyed grass — *Sisyrinchium angustifolium*

BLUE-EYED GRASS is a diminutive member of the iris family, which you can tell if you look closely at the leaves: they are flat and grow from within one another just like those of larger garden irises. Each flower is open for only 1 day before closing up and developing seeds.

Identification clues: Grasslike leaves opening directly from the ground; flowers deep blue with yellow centers and 6 petal-like structures with fine points at their tips. There are several similar species in the wild.

Where found: Meadows and roadsides; from Canada south. Native.

Height: 6–12 inches.   **In bloom:** May–June.

Growing tips: *Light needs* — full sun; *soil needs* — average organic content, average moisture. If this plant is put in rich soil, it produces an abundance of leaves but few flowers. Divide every 1–2 years for vigorous plants. Keep moist throughout summer. Perennial.

CRESTED IRIS is a wonderful plant for the garden, for it is easy to grow if planted in average soil with a sloping bed for good drainage. Over the years it can spread and begin to form a dense mat of leaves and early spring flowers.

Identification clues: Short with sword-shaped leaves; flower stalks shorter than the leaves. Flowers are 3-part, blue to purple, and with a yellow 2-ridged "crest" on the spreading sepals.

Where found: Wooded slopes, moist woods, sometimes roadsides; from Indiana to Maryland and south. Native.

Height: 4–16 inches.   **In bloom:** April–May.

Growing tips: *Light needs* — full sun to part shade; *soil needs* — average organic content, low to average moisture. Planting on a slope can be ideal for drainage, and these irises do well in rock gardens. Add a light topdressing of chopped leaves in fall. Once they are planted, leave them alone and let them spread on their own. Perennial.

Crested iris — *Iris cristata*

Blue flag —
Iris versicolor

BLUE FLAG is one of our most common native irises, and its delicate blooms can be enjoyed both in the wild and in your garden. *Iris* is from a Greek word meaning "rainbow" and refers to the many colors in the genus and within flowers.

Identification clues: Grows in wet areas and has thin, swordlike leaves; flower stalk is as tall as the leaves; bloom is blue with yellow stripes on lower sepals.

Where found: Lake edges, marshes, wetlands; from Canada south to Minnesota and to Virginia. Native.

Height: 2–3 feet.   **In bloom:** May–July.

Growing tips: *Light needs* — full sun; *soil needs* — average organic content, average to high moisture. Blue flag can grow in a variety of locations, from along a stream or lake to right in the perennial garden. Perennial

Texas bluebonnet — *Lupinus texensis*

TEXAS BLUEBONNETS form one of the most spectacular wildflower displays in North America. When they are in bloom, thousands of people go by car or bicycle to view them. Highway departments have begun to plant them for beautification as well as erosion control.

Identification clues: Basal leaves on stalks with 5 leaflets at the tip; flower stalks thick with pealike blue blossoms clustered at the tip; flower buds at top of plant are white.

Where found: Plains, pastures, brushlands, roadsides; eastern Texas. Native.

Height: 6–16 inches.   **In bloom:** March–May.

Growing tips: *Light needs* — full sun; *soil needs* — average organic content, low to average moisture. Sow seeds in fall, for this plant is a winter annual, meaning it grows a rosette of leaves in fall, overwinters, then blooms in spring and dies. It self-seeds each year. Only successful in southern Midwest. Annual.

Blue flax — *Linum perenne lewisii*

BLUE FLAX is a lovely, delicate prairie flower. The blossoms are open only in the morning and then close for the rest of the day. This plant is often a component of commercial wildflower meadow mixes.

Identification clues: Small leaves close to fine stem; branches droop at tips, where blue, 5-petaled flowers are attached.

Where found: Prairies, dry fields; from northern states south. Native.

Height: 1–2 feet.   **In bloom:** June–July.

Growing tips: *Light needs* — full sun; *soil needs* — average organic content, low to average moisture. Flax can tolerate dry conditions and is perfect for a dry wildflower meadow. Perennial.

PRAIRIE LARKSPUR is one of the more common delphiniums of the Midwest. All parts of the plant are poisonous to humans and to all livestock except sheep. *Delphinium* means "dolphin" and refers to the shape of the flower buds.

Identification clues: Flowers light blue to white and with a pointed spur off the back; arranged along the tip of the stalk.

Where found: Prairies, roadsides, pastures; from Wisconsin south to Texas and Missouri. Native.

Height: 1–4 feet.   **In bloom:** May–July.

Growing tips: *Light needs* — full sun to part shade; *soil needs* — low to rich organic content, average moisture. Easily grown from seed and prefers cooler climates. May die back in hotter part of summer and then reappear in cooler months of early fall. Perennial.

Prairie larkspur — *Delphinium virescens*

Spiderwort — *Tradescantia virginiana*

SPIDERWORT is much lovelier than its name implies. Its genus name is in honor of John Tradescant, a gardener of Charles I of England. Each flower blooms for just 1 day and then the petals, rather than falling off, actually disintegrate through the action of an enzyme in the plant.

Identification clues: Leaves clasp stem at their base and are grasslike; flowers 3-petaled and clustered at tip of stem.

Where found: Fields, roadsides, woods edges, river bottoms; from northern states south to Georgia and Missouri. Native.

Height: 1–2 feet.   **In bloom:** April–July.

Growing tips: *Light needs* — full sun to part shade; *soil needs* — low to rich organic content, average moisture. Will spread aggressively in rich soil. Divide plants every 3–4 years to retain their vigor. Perennial.

New England aster —
Aster novae-angliae

NEW ENGLAND ASTER, one of the most striking of our native asters, is loved by butterflies in late fall, when other sources of nectar have gone. Cabbage whites, sulphurs, monarchs, and painted ladies all love to feed at this aster.

Identification clues: Many small, narrow leaves clasp the hairy stem at their bases; flowers daisylike, usually deep violet, and sticky beneath.

Where found: Meadows, moist thickets, roadsides; from Canada south. Native.

Height: 3–7 feet.   **In bloom:** August–October.

Growing tips: *Light needs* — full sun; *soil needs* — average organic content, average moisture. Clipping a few inches off the stems in early July will create shorter plants with more numerous, smaller blossoms. Every few years, divide plants in spring and they will stay vigorous. Perennial.

BIRD'S-FOOT VIOLET is named for the resemblance of its leaf to the toes of a bird's foot. This species is prized by wildflower lovers, for it is a delicate little plant that grows in a seemingly inhospitable environment of dry gravel and sand. As other plants move into these areas and create shade and better soil, bird's-foot violet is crowded out.

Identification clues: Deeply lobed leaves growing from base of plant; violet-colored flowers on separate stalks taller than the leaves.

Where found: Sandy areas, upland woods, roadsides; from Minnesota to Massachusetts and south. Native.

Height: 3–5 inches.   **In bloom:** April–June.

Growing tips: *Light needs* — full sun; *soil needs* — low to average organic content, low to average moisture. This plant likes to grow where few others do. It is ideal for a rock garden or dry waste space. Will self-seed. Perennial.

Bird's-foot violet — *Viola pedata*

Bluebell —
Campanula
rotundifolia

BLUEBELLS prefer to grow in little nooks and crevices in cliffs along lakes and oceans. Here they set up residence and defy all manner of weather. They are obviously not as delicate as they appear. Bluebell is a wild relative of the garden bellflower.

Identification clues: Extremely narrow leaves and a thin, wiry stem; topped by light blue, bell-like flowers.

Where found: Rocky cliffs and meadows; from Canada south to mid-Atlantic states. Native.

Height: 6–18 inches.   **In bloom:** June–September.

Growing tips: *Light needs* — full sun to part shade; *soil needs* — average organic content, low to average moisture. Plants can be divided in spring, when they are still dormant. Perennial.

Joe-Pye weed — *Eupatorium purpureum*

JOE-PYE WEED is believed to be named for a Native American, Joe Pye, who in colonial times showed the colonists how to use the plant to relieve the symptoms of typhus fever. It is a favorite of butterflies and bees in late summer and early fall.

Identification clues: Leaves in whorls of 3 or more along stiff purplish stems; flowers light purple and in large clusters at the tips of the stems.

Where found: Mostly wet meadows, thickets, along streams; from Canada south into Appalachian Mountains. Native.

Height: 2–7 feet. **In bloom:** July–September.

Growing tips: *Light needs* — full sun; *soil needs* — rich organic content, average to high moisture. These are easy plants to grow, and they get very tall by late summer, when they start to bloom. Can be divided in spring. Perennial.

MILKWEEDS contain toxins called cardiac glycosides. Insects that feed on milkweeds accumulate these in their bodies and are then distasteful to predators such as birds and reptiles. These insects are often black combined with red or orange, colors that warn predators of their distastefulness. Examples include milkweed bugs, milkweed beetles, and monarch butterflies.

Identification clues: Large, oval leaves paired along stem; spherical clusters of small flowers at stem tips. Milky juice exudes from broken leaves or stems.

Where found: Fields, roadsides, waste spaces; from Canada south. Native.

Height: 3–5 feet. **In bloom:** June–August.

Growing tips: *Light needs* — full sun; *soil needs* — low to rich organic content, average moisture. Spreads by rhizomes that send up new shoots several feet from parent plant. Perennial.

Common milkweed — *Asclepias syriaca*

Queen-of-the-prairie — *Filipendula rubra*

QUEEN-OF-THE-PRAIRIE lives up to its name with a regal stature and elegant blooms. Native Americans are supposed to have used the plant to help cure ailments of the heart, including those of love.

Identification clues: Deeply lobed, toothed leaves; open sprays of fragrant pink blossoms at tips of stems.

Where found: Moist meadows and prairies; from Iowa to western Pennsylvania and south. Native.

Height: 3–6 feet. **In bloom:** June–August.

Growing tips: *Light needs* — full sun to part shade; *soil needs* — rich organic content, average moisture. Forms a slowly spreading clump with rosettes of leaves at the ends of short rhizomes. These can be divided from the parent plant in spring or fall. Perennial.

PRAIRIE SMOKE is also sometimes called grampa's whiskers. Both names refer to the lovely seedheads, which have soft, feathery plumes projecting from them. The plant is well adapted to dry areas and so is a good one for areas where water conservation is needed.

Identification clues: Long, feathery leaves grow from base; separate flower stalks topped by drooping, purplish flowers.

Where found: Prairies and dry, rocky meadows; from British Columbia and Ontario south to Iowa and Illinois. Native.

Height: 8–18 inches.

In bloom: April–June.

Growing tips: *Light needs* — full sun; *soil needs* — average organic content, low to average moisture. There must be good drainage around the roots. Spreads by rhizomes and can form crescent-shaped clumps. Can be divided in late summer. Perennial.

Prairie smoke — *Geum triflorum*

Wild bleeding heart — *Dicentra eximia*

BLEEDING HEART is a superb plant for the perennial garden, for it blooms throughout the summer, is tolerant of shade, and has gorgeous foliage. If you carefully take a single flower and pull it apart, the pieces resemble a wine bottle, a pair of pink rabbits, a harp, and two glasses.

Identification clues: Leaves finely cut; flowers resemble little red hearts suspended along the tip of a flower stalk.

Where found: Rocky woods; along the Appalachian Mountains from New York south. Native.

Height: 1½–2 feet.

In bloom: April–September.

Growing tips: *Light needs* — part shade to shade; *soil needs* — rich organic content, average moisture. Can tolerate sun in cooler climates but is not as luxuriant in foliage. Will increase size as a clump and can be divided in spring or fall. Perennial.

Wild bergamot — *Monarda fistulosa*

BERGAMOTS are in the mint family, and their crushed leaves release a pleasant scent. The flowers of this species vary a great deal in color, from white to rose to pink to purple. Butterflies are strongly attracted to the flowers.

Identification clues: Square stem and opposite, toothed leaves; flowers generally pink to lavender, tubular, and at the top of the stem.

Where found: Dry fields, roadsides; from Canada south. Native.

Height: 2–3 feet.   **In bloom:** July–September.

Growing tips: *Light needs —* full sun; *soil needs —* low to rich organic content, average moisture. This plant may actually do better in slightly poor soil than in very rich soil. In the wild it grows in dry areas and so is a good plant for a water-conserving garden. Should be divided every 2–3 years. Perennial.

GERANIUM is a Greek word for "crane" and refers to the shape of the unopened seedhead, which looks like a crane's bill. When dried, the seedhead opens explosively and shoots the seeds from little curling catapults. It is only distantly related to commercially grown potted geraniums; they are from the genus *Pelargonium*.

Identification clues: Leaves 5-lobed with toothed tips; flowers with 5 separate lavender petals.

Where found: Moist, open woodlands; from Canada south. Native.

Height: 1–2 feet.   **In bloom:** April–June.

Growing tips: *Light needs —* part shade to shade; *soil needs —* average to rich organic content, average moisture. Has a thick, tough rhizome that, once established, needs no special care. Will self-seed. Perennial.

Wild geranium — *Geranium maculatum*

Fireweed — *Epilobium angustifolium*

FIREWEED is known for its habit of colonizing burned-over areas or other sites cleared of vegetation, such as ski slopes and power-line rights-of-way. Other reasons for the name may be that masses of its blooms can look like fire and its tufted seeds resemble smoke as they are shed. Young shoots can be eaten as you would asparagus.

Identification clues: A tall, leafy stalk; when in the midst of blooming it has buds at the top, 4-petaled flowers in the middle, and long, thin seedpods beneath.

Where found: Clearings and burned areas; from Canada south to Georgia and west to Iowa. Originally from Eurasia.

Height: 3–7 feet. **In bloom:** July–September.

Growing tips: *Light needs* — full sun; *soil needs* — average organic content, low to average moisture. Can be divided in fall or spring. Perennial.

New York aster — *Aster novi-belgii*

NEW YORK ASTER makes a better cut flower than New England aster because its flowers do not close up each night but remain open. Many asters at garden centers are hybrids of the New England and New York asters.

Identification clues: Many small, narrow leaves clasp the smooth stem at their bases; flowers daisylike, usually pink to lavender.

Where found: Meadows, open, wet areas; from Canada south along the Atlantic coast. Native.

Height: 1–4 feet.   **In bloom:** July–October.

Growing tips: *Light needs* — full sun; *soil needs* — average organic content, average moisture. Clipping a few inches off the stems in midsummer will create shorter plants with more numerous, smaller blossoms. Every few years, divide plants in spring, and they will stay vigorous. Perennial.

COSMOS is a staple of wildflower meadow seed mixes, for it grows rapidly and blooms over many months. It is also a great cut flower, lasting a long time in arrangements and adding a variety of soft colors.

Identification clues: Finely cut, fern-like leaves; large-petaled flowers white, pink, or white with a yellow center.

Where found: Fields, roadsides; from Canada south, mostly where planted or escaped. From Mexico.

Height: 3–5 feet.

In bloom: June–September.

Growing tips: *Light needs* — full sun; *soil needs* — low to rich organic content, average moisture. Prefers well-drained soils that are not too rich. Can grow in dry areas. Easily grown from seed and transplants well. Also self-sows. Annual.

Cosmos — *Cosmos bipinnatus*

PURPLE CONEFLOWER is a premiere prairie flower and also a welcome addition to wildflower meadows and perennial gardens. If you have several plants in your garden, you can be assured of attracting butterflies, for this is one of their favorite sources of nectar.

Identification clues: Stalk and leaves coarsely hairy; large, daisylike flower with purple ray flowers and center of dark orange disk flowers on an unbranched stalk.

Where found: Prairies and roadsides; eastern Midwest and occasionally in East. Native.

Height: 1–3 feet.

In bloom: June–October.

Growing tips: *Light needs* — full sun; *soil needs* — average organic content, low to average moisture. Mix sand in with garden soil before planting. Can be divided in spring. Perennial.

Purple coneflower — *Echinacea purpurea*

Pink lady's slipper — *Cypripedium acaule*

PINK LADY'S SLIPPER has an unusual flower that is like a funhouse tunnel for its pollinators. Bumblebees, its main pollinators, first squeeze through the slit in the flower's front, which promptly closes behind them. Then they crawl up a sticky and hairy slope where the nectar is as they head for the exit at the top of the flower. Just before they leave, their backs are scraped of old pollen from previous flowers visited and then plastered with new pollen.

Identification clues: Two large basal leaves; pink, saclike flower hanging down from the tip of a leafless stalk.

Where found: Acidic woods, sand barrens, hummocks in marshes; from Canada to the northern states and down the Appalachian Mountains to Georgia. Native.

Height: 6–15 inches.   **In bloom:** May–June.

Growing tips: *Light needs* — part shade to shade; *soil needs* — average to rich organic content, average moisture. Prefers acidic soil. Perennial. *Note:* This should not be bought, since stock for sale is dug from the wild. It should also not be transplanted unless the plants are being rescued from destruction.

Shooting star — *Dodecatheon meadia*

SHOOTING STAR is aptly named, for its little groups of flowers atop its flower stalk look like falling fireworks. The flowers can range in color from lavender to pink to white, the last considered rare by some.

Identification clues: Narrow leaves at the base; distinctive flower with petals pointing backward and ring of pollen at the flower tip.

Where found: Prairies, meadows, open woods; from Wisconsin to mid-Atlantic states and south. Native.

Height: 6–24 inches.   **In bloom:** April–June.

Growing tips: *Light needs* — full sun to part shade; *soil needs* — rich organic content, average moisture. Shooting stars need moisture during the spring growing period but can withstand drought when the leaves die back in summer and the plant goes dormant. Perennial.

SPRING BEAUTY is one of the earliest flowers to bloom in spring. Its flowers open only when it is sunny, closing at night and during cloudy weather. They also close if picked. The tuber is edible but should be left alone so others can enjoy the flowers.

Identification clues: A pair of grasslike leaves partway up the stem; white to pink petals have darker lines on them.

Where found: Moist woods; from Canada south to Georgia and Texas. Native.

Height: 6–12 inches.   **In bloom:** March–May.

Growing tips: *Light needs* — part shade to shade; *soil needs* — low to rich organic content, average moisture. Dies back and becomes dormant after blooming. Self-seeds and spreads by rhizomes. Perennial.

Spring beauty — *Claytonia virginica*

Dame's rocket — *Hesperis matronalis*

DAME'S ROCKET is in the mustard family, as its 4 petals and thin seedpods suggest. It is imported from Mediterranean countries and planted in gardens. It often persists in old garden beds or where refuse from these beds may have been discarded.

Identification clues: Large leaves at base, smaller ones along stem; 4-petaled flower with a long tube at the base; can be white, pink, or purple.

Where found: Roadsides, waste spaces; from Canada south to Pennsylvania and Iowa, further south in the Appalachian Mountains. From the Mediterranean region.

Height: 2–3 feet.   **In bloom:** May–July.

Growing tips: *Light needs* — full sun to part shade; *soil needs* — average to rich organic content, average moisture. A good garden plant, but it is a short-lived perennial and will need to be replaced every few years. Can self-seed. Perennial.

Wild lupine —
Lupinus perennis

WILD LUPINES, which often grow in poor soil, were thought to rob the soil of nutrients and so were named after wolves, *lupus*. In fact, like many other members of the pea family, they enrich the soil by taking nitrogen from the air and fixing it in their roots. Watch the leaves, for they close around the stem each night.

Identification clues: Basal leaves palmate; tall spike covered with pealike blossoms in blue, purple, or white.

Where found: Meadows, dry hillsides, roadsides; throughout eastern states. Native.

Height: 1–2 feet. **In bloom:** May–June.

Growing tips: *Light needs* — full sun; *soil needs* — average organic content, low to average moisture. Once established, lupine has a deep taproot and cannot be easily transplanted. Plant younger specimens to start with and they will do better. Perennial.

BLAZING STAR and gay-feather are common names of a variety of species of liatris. Some species of liatris prefer to grow in prairies and dry, rocky soils; others, such as *Liatris spicata*, prefer moist meadows. Liatrises are a favorite flower of adult butterflies, which come to drink the nectar.

Identification clues: Grasslike leaves beneath; tall spikes with lavender to purple feathery flowers at the top.

Where found: Meadows, roadsides; from southern New York to Michigan and south. Native.

Height: 2–5 feet.

In bloom: August–September.

Growing tips: *Light needs* — full sun; *soil needs* — average organic content, low to average moisture. This species likes a little more moisture than many other species of liatris, which can grow in dry situations. Good for meadows, wet meadows, and perennial gardens. Detach small corms from the larger corm in spring to propagate. Perennial.

Blazing star — *Liatris spicata*

Ironweed — *Vernonia noveboracensis*

IRONWEED is a good plant for a wildflower meadow where the ground is a little soggy, such as a swale or the edge of a brook. The genus is named for William Vernon, an English botanist who visited North America. A closely related species is tall ironweed, *V. altissima*, which grows to 10 feet tall.

Identification clues: Toothed, narrow leaves alternate on stem; feathery, violet flowers terminate branches at top of stem.

Where found: Streambanks, moist meadows, roadside ditches; from Ohio to Massachusetts and south. Native.

Height: 3–7 feet.   **In bloom:** August–October.

Growing tips: *Light needs* — full sun; *soil needs* — low to rich organic content, average moisture. Does best in moist to wet soil. Spreads by short rhizomes. Can be divided in spring or late fall. Perennial.

Glossary

Alternate leaves: Leaves growing singly on alternate sides of the stem.

Basal leaves: Leaves near the ground at the base of a plant.

Basal rosette: Compressed whorl of leaves that radiate from a central point at the base of the stem.

Bracts: A small, leaflike appendage on a stem or flower.

Compound leaves: Large leaves composed of many smaller leaflets.

Corm: An underground swollen portion of a stem.

Disk flowers: Clusters of numerous tiny flowers on the central part of a Composite family flower, such as the center of an oxeye daisy.

Flowerhead: A grouping of many small flowers into one bunch on the top of a stem.

Leaf axil: The point between the stem and the base of the leaf attachment.

Leaf scars: A small mark left on a plant stem showing the point where a shed leaf was formerly attached.

Opposite leaves: Leaves growing in pairs opposite each other on the stem.

Palmate: In an arrangement like the fingers of a hand.

Pistil: The total female reproductive organ in the flower, made up of the egg, ovary, style, and stigma.

Ray flowers: Individual flowers with a long, straplike petal that are usually on the edge of a flowerhead, such as those around the edge of an oxeye daisy.

Rhizome: An underground stem that often grows horizontally and may produce new stems.

Rosette: Compressed whorl of leaves that radiate from a central point above the roots.

Runner: An above-ground stem that, when it touches the ground, may grow roots and possibly a new stem.

Sepal: One of an outer whorl of leaflike structures that enclose the flower at the bud stage.

Stamen: The whole male reproductive organ in the flower, made up of the filament and the anther.

Tuber: A swelling on a rhizome that usually stores food.

Resources

Books on Wildflowers

Art, Henry W. 1986. *A Garden of Wildflowers.* Pownal, VT: Storey Communications, Inc.

Martin, Laura C. 1986. *The Wildflower Meadow Book.* Charlotte, NC: East Woods Press.

National Wildflower Research Center. 1989. *Wildflower Handbook.* Austin, TX: Texas Monthly Press.

Newcomb, Lawrence. 1977. *Newcomb's Wildflower Guide.* Boston: Little, Brown and Company.

Peterson, Roger T., and Margaret McKenny. 1968. *A Field Guide to Wildflowers.* Boston: Houghton Mifflin Company.

Phillips, Harry R. 1985. *Growing and Propagating Wildflowers.* Chapel Hill: University of North Carolina Press.

Smith, J. Robert and Beatrice S. 1980. *The Prairie Garden.* Madison: University of Wisconsin Press.

Sperka, Marie. 1984. *Growing Wildflowers: A Gardener's Guide.* New York: Charles Scribner's Sons.

Wildflower Seed Mixes

Alternative Groundcovers, Inc. P.O. Box 49092, Colorado Springs, CO 80949. 719-548-1471.

Applewood Seed Company. 5380 Vivian Street, Arvada, CO 80002. 303-431-6283.

W. Atlee Burpee Company. 300 Park Avenue, Warminster, PA 18974. 215-674-4915.

Clyde Robin Seed. P.O. Box 2366, Castro Valley, CA 18974. 415-785-0425.

Harris Seeds. P.O. Box 22960, Rochester, NY 14624. 716-442-9386.

Johnny's Selected Seeds. Foss Hill Road, Albion, ME 04910. 207-437-9294.

Lofts Seed, Inc. P.O. Box 146, Bound Brook, NJ 08805. 800-526-3890.

Park Seed Company, Inc. Cokesbury Road, Greenwood, SC 29647. 803-223-7333.

Passiflora. Route 1, Box 190-A, Germantown, NC 27019.

Prairie Moon Nursery. Route 3, Box 163, Winona, MN 55987. 507-452-5231.

Prairie Nursery. P.O. Box 306, Westfield, WI 53964. 608-296-3679.

Prairie Restorations, Inc. P.O. Box 327, Princeton, MN 55371. 612-389-4342.

Prairie Seed Source. P.O. Box 83, North Lake, WI 53064.

Stock Seed Farms. Route 1, Box 112, Murdock, NE 68407. 800-759-1520.

Vermont Wildflower Farm. Route 7, Charlotte, VT 05445.

White Swan Ltd. 8104 Southwest Nimbus Avenue, Beaverton, OR 90075.

Good Plant Sources

For a list of nurseries that are responsible sellers of native plants, buy the book *Nursery Sources: Native Plants and Wildflowers*, published by the New England Wildflower Society, Hemenway Road, Framingham, MA 01701. 508-877-7630.

Native Plant Societies

Alabama Wildflower Society. Route 2, Box 115, Northport, AL 35476. 205-339-2511.

Arkansas Native Plant Society. Department of Forest Resources, University of Arkansas–Monticello, Monticello, AR 71655. 501-367-2835.

Canadian Wildflower Society. 35 Bauer Crescent, Unionville, ONT L3R 4H3.

Cincinnati Wildflower Preservation Society. Department of Biology, University of Cincinnati, Cincinnati, OH 45221.

Florida Native Plant Society. 1133 West Morse Blvd., Suite 201, Winter Park, FL 32789. 305-647-8839.

Florida Native Plant Society, Suncoast Chapter. Seffner, FL 33584.

Illinois Native Plant Society. Department of Botany, Southern Illinois University, Carbondale, IL 62901. 618-536-2331.

Kansas Wildflower Society. Mulvane Art Center, Washburn University, Topeka, KS 66621.

Kentucky Native Plant Society. Department of Biological Sciences, Eastern Kentucky University, Richmond, KY 40475. 606-622-6257.

Louisiana Native Plant Society. C/o Richard Johnson, Route 1, Box 151, Saline, LA 71070.

Louisiana Project Wildflower. Lafayette Natural History Museum, 637 Girard Park Drive, Lafayette, LA 70503. 318-261-8350.

Maryland Native Plant Society. 14720 Claude Lane, Silver Spring, MD 20904. 301-236-4124.

Minnesota Native Plant Society. 220 Biological Science Center, 1445 Gortner Avenue, St. Paul, MN 55108.

Mississippi Native Plant Society. C/o Travis Salley, 202 North Andrews Avenue, Cleveland, MS 38732. 601-843-2330.

Missouri Native Plant Society. Box 6612, Jefferson City, MO 65102. 816-429-4933.

Missouri Prairie Foundation. Box 200, Columbia, MO 65205.

National Wildflower Research Center. 2600 FM 973 North, Austin, TX 78725.

Native Plant Society of Texas. Box 23836 — TWU Station, Denton, TX 76204. 817-627-2862.

New England Wildflower Society. Hemenway Road, Framingham, MA 01701. 508-877-7630.

New England Wildflower Society, Maine Chapter. 107 Nichols Street, Topsham, ME 04086. 207-782-5238.

New Jersey Native Plant Society. Frelinghuysen Arboretum, Box 1295 R, Morristown, NJ 07960. 201-377-3956.

North Carolina Wildflower Preservation Society. North Carolina Botanical Garden, UNC-CH Totten Center 457-A, Chapel Hill, NC 27514.

Ohio Native Plant Society. 6 Louise Drive, Chagrin Falls, OH 44022. 216-338-6622.

Oklahoma Native Plant Society. 2435 South Peoria Avenue, Tulsa, OK 74114. 918-749-6401.

Operation Wildflower, Central Atlantic Division. 2513 Raven Road, Wilmington, DE 19810.

Pennsylvania Native Plant Society. 1806 Commonwealth Building, 316 Fourth Avenue, Pittsburgh, PA 15222.

Pensacola Wildflower Society. C/o Jim Dyehouse, 3911 Dunwoody Drive, Pensacola, FL 32503.

Tennessee Native Plant Society. Department of Botany, University of Tennessee, Knoxville, TN 37996. 615-974-2256.

Virginia Wildflower Preservation Society. Box 844, Annandale, VA 22003. 703-356-7425.

West Virginia Native Plant Society. Herbarium — Brooks Hall, West Virginia University, Morgantown, WV 26506.

Index to the Gallery of Wildflowers